Comments on other *Amazing Stories* from readers & reviewers

"Tightly written volumes filled with lots of wit and humour about famous and infamous Canadians."
Eric Shackleton, *The Globe and Mail*

"The heightened sense of drama and intrigue, combined with a good dose of human interest is what sets Amazing Stories *apart."*
Pamela Klaffke, *Calgary Herald*

"This is popular history as it should be... For this price, buy two and give one to a friend."
Terry Cook, a reader from Ottawa, on ***Rebel Women***

"Glasner creates the moment of the explosion itself in graphic detail...she builds detail upon gruesome detail to create a convincingly authentic picture."
Peggy McKinnon, *The Sunday Herald,* on ***The Halifax Explosion***

"It was wonderful...I found I could not put it down. I was sorry when it was completed."
Dorothy F. from Manitoba on ***Marie-Anne Lagimodière***

"Stories are rich in description, and bristle with a clever, stylish realness."
Mark Weber, *Central Alberta Advisor,* on ***Ghost Town Stories II***

"A compelling read. Bertin...has selected only the most intriguing tales, which she narrates with a wealth of detail."
Joyce Glasner, *New Brunswick Reader,* on ***Strange Events***

"The resulting book is one readers will want to share with all the women in their lives."
Lynn Martel, *Rocky Mountain Outlook,* on ***Wom***

AMAZING STORIES

GREAT CANADIAN WAR HEROES

AMAZING STORIES

GREAT CANADIAN WAR HEROES

Victoria Cross Recipients of World War II

HISTORY/MILITARY

by Tom Douglas

PUBLISHED BY ALTITUDE PUBLISHING CANADA LTD.
1500 Railway Avenue, Canmore, Alberta T1W 1P6
www.altitudepublishing.com
1-800-957-6888

First published 2005

Publisher	Stephen Hutchings
Associate Publisher	Kara Turner
Series Editor	Jill Foran
Editor	Yvonne Van Ruskenveld
Digital Photo Colouring	Bryan Pezzi

We acknowledge the financial support of the Government of Canada through the Book Publishing Industry Development Program (BPIDP) for our publishing activities.

Altitude GreenTree Program
Altitude Publishing will plant twice as many trees as were used in the manufacturing of this product.

We acknowledge the support of the Canada Council for the Arts which in 2003 invested $21.7 million in writing and publishing throughout Canada.

Canada Council for the Arts | Conseil des Arts du Canada

National Library of Canada Cataloguing in Publication Data

Douglas, Tom, 1941-
Great Canadian war heroes / Tom Douglas.

(Amazing stories)
Includes bibliographical references.
ISBN 1-55439-057-5

1. Victoria Cross. 2. World War, 1939-1945--Biography. 3. Canada--Armed Forces--Biography. 4. Heroes--Canada--Biography. I. Title. II. Series: Amazing stories (Canmore, Alta.)

CR4885.D68 2005 940.54'0092'271
C2005-901534-9

Printed and bound in Canada by Friesens
4 6 8 9 7 5 3

To Marion & Archie…
For giving me a silver mine!

Contents

Prologue

Corporal Fred Topham — "Toppy" to his buddies — watched in horror as two other medical orderlies were cut down by machine-gun fire as they tried to help a wounded soldier in an open field.

Toppy could hear the injured paratrooper's cries for help above the gunfire, and he couldn't stand it any longer. Without waiting for orders, he began running a zigzag course toward the downed soldier, ignoring the bullets that whizzed over his head and ploughed up the ground all around him.

Reaching the disabled paratrooper, Toppy realized the man needed immediate first aid if he was going to survive being dragged or carried out of the danger zone. As he worked on the wounded man, Toppy was shot in the face. Ignoring the intense bleeding and excruciating pain, he did all he could for the soldier, then hoisted him onto his broad shoulders and staggered through continuous heavy fire to the shelter of a wooded area.

Refusing treatment for his own wound, Toppy administered first aid to dozens of other injured Canadian soldiers for several hours. Finally agreeing that he too needed medical help, Toppy started back to his company command post. But he heard cries for help, this time from within a disabled vehicle.

A motorized Bren gun carrier had taken a direct hit from German mortars and was engulfed in flames. The wreckage was loaded with live ammunition, and a British officer had ordered everyone to stay clear.

Toppy couldn't stand by while his comrades-in-arms perished right there in front of him. Despite shouts of protest from the other onlookers, Toppy once again dashed through German mortar fire and reached the carrier.

One by one, he dragged three wounded soldiers from the exploding vehicle and brought them to safety. Only then did he allow the painful wound on his face to be treated.

Introduction Total Victory

orld War II, a horrible, bloody conflict, resulted in the worldwide loss of an estimated 55 million lives. More than half of the fatalities were civilians, with countless millions more left homeless. Hostilities began when Nazi dictator Adolf Hitler broke his word to Great Britain's hapless Prime Minister Neville Chamberlain, hurling his stormtroopers and killing machines at a virtually defenceless Poland on September 1, 1939.

Grasping Hitler's coattails, Italy's Benito Mussolini strutted into the fray soon after, creating the German-Italian alliance known as the Axis. A little over two years later, the Japanese joined forces with the Axis powers, bringing the Americans into the war on the Allied side with an attack on the US fleet at Pearl Harbor on December 7, 1941.

Canada declared war on Germany on September 10, 1939, and, by the time hostilities ceased almost six years later, more than 42,000 Canadians had been killed in action or died later of wounds sustained in battle. Tens of thousands more returned to their homeland wounded in body or spirit.

Toward the end of April 1945, the German military juggernaut, defeated at sea and in the air, saw its once seemingly invincible army crushed between the pincers of the Russian hordes to the east and Allied troops to the west. On April 25, American and Russian troops met at the Elbe River, which ran through a war-ravaged Germany, signifying the end of the Nazi attempt to conquer the free world. Hitler had boasted of founding an empire — his so-called Third Reich — that would last 1000 years. It lay shattered in the ruins of Berlin within a dozen years of the 1933 Nazi takeover of the German Parliament.

At about the same time as the Americans and Russians were fraternizing on the Elbe, Canadian military leaders were negotiating a temporary cease-fire with the German occupying forces in Holland. Aware that the Nazis were allowing the Dutch population to slowly starve to death, the Canadians delivered an ultimatum. If they weren't allowed to deliver supplies to the enslaved population of the Netherlands, the German military leaders in the area would be tried as war criminals as soon as hostilities ceased.

The Nazi Reichskommissar in Holland capitulated, and fighting ceased on April 28. Almost immediately, convoys of food and supplies dropped from RCAF bombers began reaching the ravaged people of the Netherlands, who had been subsisting — and in many cases dying — on an average intake of 320 calories a day. Much of their meagre supply of food had consisted of tulip bulbs and whatever could be scraped out of garbage cans with a spoon.

On April 30, 1945, Hitler, his mistress, Eva Braun, and several high-ranking Nazis committed suicide in his Berlin bunker. Hitler's successor, Admiral Karl Doenitz, dispatched General Alfred Jodl to the Supreme Headquarters Allied Expeditionary Forces (SHAEF) detachment in the French city of Rheims to seek terms for an end to the war. On May 7, General Jodl signed the papers for an unconditional surrender to take place the next day.

General Walter Bedell Smith, chief of staff for Supreme Allied Commander General Dwight D. Eisenhower, signed the peace treaty for the Allied Expeditionary Force. General Eisenhower's absence is widely regarded as his reaction to a recent tour of several Nazi concentration camps. It has been suggested that he was so disgusted by the evidence he saw of atrocities perpetrated against the inmates that he refused to be in the same room with the surrendering German officers. This was considered a slap in the face to the "by-the-book" German High Command, who had to be content with an underling dictating the terms of surrender.

Meanwhile, Canadian General Charles Foulkes had already accepted the surrender of German troops in Holland on May 5 in the village of Wageningen while his colleague

General Guy Simonds had done the same on his front in the German seaside resort town of Bad Zwischenahn.

With the cessation of hostilities on May 8, 1945 — known from that day forward as VE (Victory in Europe) Day — members of the Royal Canadian Army, Royal Canadian Navy, Royal Canadian Air Force, and Canadian Merchant Navy began looking forward to a triumphal return to their home and native land.

Some stayed on to finish the job in the Far East, where hostilities ended on VJ (Victory in Japan) Day, August 15, 1945. The vast majority of Canadian troops, however, had fought in the European theatre of operations, and the monumental task of demobilizing them back to Canada went on for months after Germany's surrender.

Among those returning home was a handful of men who had been awarded the Victoria Cross (VC). Only 16 Canadian combatants in World War II had been so honoured, and, of those, eight returned to Canada after the war. The remaining eight had paid the supreme sacrifice in battle.

Thousands of other Canadians won medals during the hostilities, and countless thousands more performed heroic deeds that went unrewarded because there was no one left alive to attest to their courage. Above all, these 16 Victoria Cross winners remain as symbols of the indomitable Canadian spirit in times of turmoil.

They were truly amazing individuals (only one survives as of this writing) and theirs, without a doubt, are truly amazing stories, told here in chronological order based on the action for which they received the British Commonwealth's highest award.

1941

Sergeant-Major John Robert Osborn: No Greater Love

Company Sergeant-Major John Osborn, by all rights, shouldn't have been fighting in that battle against the Japanese on a hill in Hong Kong on the morning of December 19, 1941. In the first place, he was 42 years of age. On top of that, he was a married man with five children. And he had already paid his dues by serving in World War I in two different branches of the service.

As a 17-year-old seaman in the Royal Naval Volunteer Reserve, the British-born Osborn saw action in May 1916 at the Battle of Jutland, billed as the largest naval battle of the Great War. He later joined the Royal Marines and was gassed while fighting on Europe's Western Front.

Osborn was born in a horse-drawn caravan at Foulden, England, on January 2, 1899, the son of itinerant peddlers who frequented the fairs and markets throughout the area. Returning to England after his war service, Osborn was advised by a family doctor that his damaged lungs would respond best to fresh air and sunshine. Since these were commodities in short supply in the coalfire-induced fogs of England, Osborn emigrated to Canada in 1920.

After two years as a farmhand in Saskatchewan, he moved to Manitoba where he joined the maintenance division of the Canadian Pacific Railway and settled down to what he had reason to believe would be a long, happy married life in his adopted country.

Osborn joined the Winnipeg Grenadiers as a part-time soldier in 1933 and was called to active service one week before Canada declared war on Germany in September 1939. Canadian troops early in the war found themselves short on equipment and training, but the British High Command was desperate for reinforcements for their Hong Kong garrison. When they assured the Canadian government that the troops would be no more than window dressing to deter the Japanese from attacking the island colony, the Grenadiers and the Royal Rifles of Canada, just under 2000 strong, shipped out.

The sea voyage from Vancouver, BC, to Hong Kong took three weeks in the cramped confines of the MV *Awatea,* a former inter-city ferry that had only recently been converted into a troopship. When the Canadians arrived on November 16, 1941, their jubilant welcome by the grateful residents of

Hong Kong was overshadowed by the discovery that much of their equipment, including more than 200 vehicles, had been shipped elsewhere. The news would get worse — and very quickly.

On December 7, 1941, the Japanese attacked the United States' Hawaii-based fleet at Pearl Harbor. Suddenly, the British, Canadian, and Indian troops in Hong Kong found themselves defending what was now considered a strategic target in the Japanese battle plan for military control of the Pacific. Many of the Grenadiers had been raw recruits with no combat experience just six months beforehand. Now, they would be facing a formidable enemy as the first Canadian troops to do battle in World War II.

Shortly after news of the Pearl Harbor attack reached Hong Kong, about 50 Japanese warplanes pulverized the island's Kai Tek Airport, destroying the five antiquated aircraft — two Walrus amphibians and three Wildebeest Torpedo bombers — that comprised British air support for Hong Kong's defence. Hot on the heels of this attack came word that Japanese troops had crossed over the Chinese border to the north and were rapidly advancing toward Hong Kong.

The next bit of devastating news was that the bombing of the American fleet at Pearl Harbor, the sinking of two British warships off Singapore, and the destruction of the Royal Air Force planes at Kai Tek meant there would be no air or sea cover to defend the colony.

On December 18, the Japanese began landing massive

numbers of troops on the north-east shore of the island, and, within hours, had captured several strategic sites, including the 436-metre Mount Butler at the island's centre.

The Hong Kong defenders woke up to a cool, grey, and misty December 19. The orders of the day instructed Osborn's company of Grenadiers to retake Mount Butler. They threw everything they had into the assault, advancing slowly up the steep, rain-drenched bluffs under heavy enemy firepower. The Grenadiers finally attacked the Japanese at the mountain summit in a bayonet charge, suffering tremendous casualties from the hail of leaden fire poured into their ranks from entrenched Japanese machine guns.

There are several conjectures as to why the Grenadiers chose to attack a heavily fortified position with bayonets — known in military jargon as the weapon of last resort. For one thing, the Canadians were short of ammunition. And they had been falsely informed during training sessions on their trans-Pacific voyage that the Japanese were small, weak, badly fed and poorly equipped soldiers with low morale who would turn and run under close combat conditions. It had also been drilled into the recruits that a bayonet charge is one of the most frightening acts an enemy can face.

Whatever led to the decision, the use of "the brave man's weapon" allowed the Canadians to rout the Japanese from the top of Mount Butler, but at a tremendous cost, with most of the Grenadiers' senior officers killed and their company's strength drastically reduced.

The Canadians managed to hold onto the summit of Mount Butler for three hours, but the Japanese moved three companies of battle-hardened troops of the Imperial Army against them, forcing them to withdraw.

Osborn and a small band of Grenadiers covered the retreat of their 30 or so surviving comrades. When it came time for the few remaining Canadians to leave the area, Osborn was the last to go, running a gauntlet of heavy rifle and machine-gun fire and assisting stragglers as they staggered back to a new position.

Later that day, Osborn's decimated company was cut off from the rest of the battalion and completely surrounded by the Japanese. Enemy troops were able to get close enough to the Grenadiers to throw hand grenades into their position — a slight depression in the hillside into which the embattled Canadians had crowded. Several of these missiles landed at the sergeant-major's feet, and he quickly scooped them up and lobbed them back at the Japanese.

Finally, one grenade landed just beyond Osborn's reach. Realizing that it was impossible to get to the sputtering bomb in time, he shouted a warning to his men and threw himself on the grenade just as it exploded. Osborn was killed instantly, but his selfless act saved the lives of the Grenadiers in the immediate vicinity.

While Osborn's instinctive reaction was without question a brave deed, this courageous soldier may have died in vain. The six surviving members of the two platoons of "A" company of the Winnipeg Grenadiers were eventually overwhelmed, as were the other Hong Kong defenders, and they became prisoners of war.

Many of their comrades had been wounded, and the captured soldiers asked the victorious Japanese if they could take the injured men with them. The Japanese officers refused, saying they would take care of the wounded, which they did by shooting or bayoneting all of them to death.

After the war, a war crimes investigation unit found the remains of the men in a streambed. Japanese Colonel Tanaka Ryosabura, whose men had slaughtered the helpless Allied wounded, was tried, convicted, and executed for his crimes.

The battle of Hong Kong resulted in the death of 290 Canadians and the wounding of 493 more. Almost as many died later due to the brutal forced march they were subjected to or as a result of the unbelievably harsh and inhumane conditions in the Japanese prison camps.

News of Sergeant-Major Osborn's heroic self-sacrifice did not surface until after the war, when the few surviving members of "A" company were released from Japanese prison camps and were at last able to tell the tale. Ironically, while Osborn's actions were the first of the war to earn a Victoria Cross for a member of the Canadian Armed Forces, his medal was the last to be awarded because of the time lag between when he was killed and when the authorities learned of his brave deed.

Due to the nature of his death and the time lapse before the Allies regained the battle area, Sergeant-Major Osborn's remains were never recovered, and he has no known grave. However, his name appears on Column 25 of the Sai Wan Memorial in Hong Kong. His medal is on display at the Canadian War Museum in Ottawa.

A section of the citation accompanying his Victoria Cross award reads: "Company Sergeant-Major Osborn was an inspiring example to all throughout the defence which he assisted so magnificently in maintaining against an overwhelming enemy force for over eight and a half hours, and in his death he displayed the highest quality of heroism and self-sacrifice."

1942

Reverend John Weir Foote: The Voluntary Captive

Armed with nothing more than a Bible, Reverend John Foote, an honorary captain with The Royal Hamilton Light Infantry, stepped off a landing barge into the hell that was Dieppe on August 19, 1942.

Born in Madoc, Ontario, on May 5, 1904, John Foote was the antithesis of the tough fighting man that government propagandists conjure up on recruitment posters. After attending the University of Western Ontario, Queen's University, and McGill University, he entered the Presbyterian ministry, serving congregations in Fort Coulonge, Quebec, and Port Hope, Ontario. When World War II broke out, he enlisted in the Canadian Chaplain Service. Less than three years later, he faced brutal enemy fire on the beaches of Dieppe.

There are those who claim that the raid by about 5000

Canadian soldiers on that heavily fortified French seaside port was a vital trial run that taught the Allies many valuable lessons. The argument goes that what was learned on those bloody beaches saved hundreds and perhaps thousands of lives in the D-Day landings in Normandy on June 6, 1944.

Many others consider it a suicide mission caused by a colossal series of blunders by military strategists in British Combined Operations and, in particular, by Lord Louis Mountbatten. They base their theory partly on the fact that the raid's success depended on complete surprise, yet the Germans knew the Canadians were coming and Combined Ops knew they knew.

Furthermore, Mountbatten planned the operation based on an earlier raid on the heavily fortified Atlantic port of St. Nazaire, in which most of the British commandos taking part were either killed or captured. Sending men into a strategic harbour facility where the defenders are armed to the teeth — especially when there is little if any air cover and virtually no support from naval guns offshore — is a recipe for disaster. Yet Mountbatten persisted, largely in an attempt, it is argued, to mollify the Americans and Russians who were pressing for a second front to take pressure off the Nazi-harassed Soviet sector in Eastern Europe. Those even less kind to Mountbatten's memory suggest that he and his superiors sent the Canadians on a suicide mission to prove to the second front proponents that such an exercise was impossible at that time.

Any post-war visitor to the Dieppe beaches will quickly surmise how perilous the terrain was that the Canadians were expected to negotiate. The Dieppe "beaches" are more like a series of three steep hills covered in boulders ranging in size from small ball bearings to baseballs. Tanks that took part in the raid became bogged down as their treads failed to gain purchase on the loose rocks. Those invaders who managed to straggle ashore through a hail of machine-gun and mortar fire found it tough going as they tried to run uphill on the treacherously shifting stones.

If the entire force of German defenders had been blind, they probably still would have won the day by simply aiming their weapons at the beach from their dug-in positions on the chalk cliffs that straddled the landing areas. The Canadians didn't have a chance. Within three hours, the battle was lost. The staggering toll of casualties included 907 dead, many of the bodies rolling grotesquely in and out with the waves, and nearly 2000 troops taken captive.

As 38-year-old Honorary Captain Foote leapt from a landing craft into the chaos of floating bodies, wrecked equipment, and withering enemy fire, he immediately set to work taking care of the wounded. War correspondent Terence Robertson wrote in *Maclean's* magazine that Foote saved at least 30 lives. His first action was to lift a wounded soldier onto his back and wade to the nearest boat, persuading those around him to help load the injured man on board. "Every man carry a man," he shouted through the din of battle, urging others to go to the aid of the wounded.

All through the battle, Foote ministered to the injured at the makeshift regimental aid post. Time and again he left the relative safety of this shelter to inject morphine, give first aid, say a prayer for the dead and dying, or carry the wounded back to the aid station.

When the tide began to go out, the regimental aid post was moved to the shelter of a stranded landing craft. Rev. Foote continued to expose himself to a storm of enemy fire by dashing between the aid station and the beach to guide, carry, or drag wounded soldiers to safety. When German shells set the ammunition in the landing craft on fire, the padre risked his life once more by pulling the wounded out of the inferno, despite the fact that an explosion could happen at any moment.

When rescue craft appeared offshore, Foote transferred the wounded one by one through water crimson with blood and churned up by enemy mortar and machine-gun fire. Several times he was exhorted to climb aboard a vessel heading to safety but he steadfastly refused while there were still wounded on shore who needed his help.

Finally, when he could do nothing more for the fallen, he was persuaded to climb aboard a retreating landing craft to be taken back to a Canadian ship offshore. As the small boat pulled away from the carnage, however, Foote leapt back into the water and headed once again for the beach.

The padre would later explain his action this way: "It

Reverend John Weir Foote

seemed to me the men ashore would need me far more in captivity than any of those going home." Thus, Rev. John Foote walked staunchly into a hopeless situation where capture was inevitable. Without thought for his own well-being, he willingly became a prisoner of war, spending the next two years and nine months in a German prison camp.

When he was released on May 5, 1945, by the British Grenadier Guards, Rev. Foote elected to stay in the service until 1948. At that time he returned to Canada and, like another Dieppe prisoner, Lieutenant-Colonel Cec Merritt, decided to enter politics.

Rev. Foote was first elected to the Ontario Legislature on June 7, 1948, and served until May 4, 1959. He was appointed minister of reform institutions in 1950 and remained in that Cabinet post for almost seven years.

Rev. Foote made his home in Cobourg, Ontario, until his death on May 2, 1988. He is buried in the town's St. Andrew's Cemetery. Prior to his death, he donated his Victoria Cross and other medals to the Royal Hamilton Light Infantry.

The citation accompanying Rev. Foote's VC award talks of his courage during the Dieppe Raid. It reads, in part: "Honourary Captain Foote personally saved many lives by his efforts and his example inspired all around him. Those who observed him state that the calmness of this heroic officer as he walked about, collecting the wounded on the fire-swept beach, will never be forgotten."

Lieutenant-Colonel Charles Cecil Ingersoll Merritt: Getting Even

Lieutenant-Colonel "Cec" Merritt took one look at the bodies of Canadian soldiers piling up on the unprotected bridge over the River Scie near the Dieppe landing site and decided that drastic action had to be taken.

The 32-year-old commanding officer of the South Saskatchewan Regiment turned to his anxious troops and urged them forward, strolling out onto the battered bridge. Eyewitnesses would later suggest that Merritt acted as though he was ambling onto a small span over an inlet at Vancouver's Stanley Park rather than a strategic structure that the Dieppe attackers desperately needed to secure.

"What's the matter with you fellows?" he shouted back at his men. "You're not frightened are you? Come on over! There's nothing to worry about here."

War correspondent Wallace Reyburn, in a CBC radio broadcast covering the disastrous raid on the French resort and fishing village of Dieppe on August 19, 1942, gave a vivid eyewitness account of Lieutenant-Colonel Merritt's heroic leadership on that fateful morning.

Reyburn estimated that the bridge was about 180 metres long and was more of a causeway, wide-beamed and without railings. Compounding the danger of there being nothing to hide behind once the soldiers started across the span was the presence of a high concrete fort on a hill across the river. All of its guns were trained on the bridge.

But the river was in full flood and the bridge was the only way to get across, other than swimming for it, which again would expose the Canadians to enemy gunfire.

As the first Canadian soldiers started across the bridge, the Germans let loose with rifles, machine guns, and mortars. Huge shards of concrete, dislodged by exploding mortar shells, flew in all directions. Bullets ricocheted off the roadway. Within minutes, the span was riddled with craters and bullet holes, and covered with the bodies of dead Canadians.

It was at this point that Lieutenant-Colonel Merritt strode up the hill to get a closer look at the action. It was a very warm day and he casually removed his helmet to wipe the sweat from his forehead. As he did so, he asked for a report on the situation. He was told that the Saskatchewans had hit a roadblock of brutal enemy fire and were unable to cross the bridge. After taking a moment to analyze the situation, he announced calmly what he planned to do.

"Now men," the CBC correspondent heard him say, "we're going to get across. Follow me. Don't bunch up together, spread out. Here we go!"

As if he didn't have a care in the world, Merritt sauntered onto the bridge, his steel helmet dangling from his wrist. Mesmerized by this show of courage, some of his men followed in his wake.

The CBC's Reyburn heaped praise on the Saskatchewans' commanding officer in filing a report back to Canada. "As I watched him lead his men through that thundering barrage, I felt a quiver run up and down my spine. I'd never seen anything like it."

This action was heroic in itself, but Merritt repeated the feat three more times. Showing total disregard for the German firepower, he walked through a heavy barrage of mortar and light arms fire that rained down on the bridge.

Once his men were across the causeway, he called for an advance on the village of Pourville just up the road, only to have his troops brought up short against concrete pillboxes spewing deadly machine-gun bullets in their path.

Once again, Lieutenant-Colonel Merritt led the charge, knocking out one pillbox himself by getting close enough to throw hand grenades through its firing ports. When the enemy guns in that sector of the fighting had been silenced, it was discovered that Merritt had been wounded twice. His battalion had been reduced to fewer than 300 men.

Still he refused to give up. The South Saskatchewans' orders for the Dieppe raid had been to take Pourville, on the west side of the port, then the cliffs above the village. It was a bold plan under ideal circumstances, and virtually impossible once the raid had gone horribly wrong.

With disaster all around, Merritt improvised a perimeter at the north end of the bridge with whatever Canadian troops he could muster under the chaotic conditions in the battle area. He faced another crisis when the soldiers who had been designated as runners between sections of the perimeter were all killed. Merritt himself, despite his wounds, dodged enemy fire time and again to keep in touch with his section leaders, taking shelter wherever he could behind burned-out vehicles and the debris of shattered German gun emplacements.

But his hopes for holding on until reinforcements arrived to help him reach the Pourville objective were dashed when he finally received orders to pull out. The Dieppe raid was a fiasco caused by bad luck and poor planning. The decision had been made to withdraw as many troops as possible in order to attack Hitler's Fortress Europe at another place and another time.

Still, Merritt was not through fighting on that disastrous day. He stalked a German sniper with a Bren gun and silenced him. He then began collecting weapons, announcing coolly that he would be staying behind to hold off the enemy while his men attempted to reach the landing craft on the beach and escape back to England.

He was last heard telling one of his men that he was going to "get even" with the Nazis on behalf of all his dead comrades. Years later, he would make light of his actions by stating that he didn't know what else to do since "we were not in a position to take Paris."

The South Saskatchewan battalion left 84 dead on the Dieppe beaches while 89 more, including Merritt and 8 other officers, were taken prisoner and loaded onto cattle cars to be transported to German prison camps.

Lieutenant-Colonel Merritt ended up in camp Oflag VIIB in Bavaria where he and 64 other POWs escaped through a tunnel in early June 1943. A few managed to evade recapture, but Merritt was not one of them. He returned to 14 days of solitary confinement and remained a POW until US forces overran the prison camp in April 1945.

He was not very proud of the fact that he had been taken prisoner, suggesting after he had been freed that others had had a much rougher time of it. "My war lasted six hours," he was quoted as saying. "There are plenty of Canadians who went all the way from the landings in Sicily to the very end." Of his time as a POW, he said: "It was an enforced idleness. It cannot be translated into virtue."

Merritt's toughness in the face of the enemy was part of his heritage. His father was a Canadian Army officer who was killed at the Second Battle of Ypres on April 23, 1915, just seven years after Merritt's birth in Vancouver, BC, on November 10, 1908.

Cec Merritt enjoyed a long and illustrious life after being released from the German prison camp. While still a POW, he was nominated "in absentia" as the federal Progressive Conservative candidate for the riding of Vancouver-Burrard. And while he hadn't earlier been "in a position to take Paris," this time he tasted victory by winning the election. Great-grandson of Sir Charles Tupper (a Father of Confederation and an early prime minister of Canada), Merritt spent three years representing his constituents in Ottawa. Following the loss of his seat in the general election of 1948, he returned to his pre-war law practice.

In 1951, he was appointed commanding officer of the Seaforth Highlanders of Canada (R), a post he held for three years. Throughout his lifetime, he had a close association with the Vancouver Police Commission, Royal Canadian Legion, Boy Scouts of Canada, and the BC Corps of Commissionaires.

Lt.Col. Merritt steadfastly refused to join in the

widespread criticism of the Dieppe raid. "We were very glad to go," he told an interviewer. "We were delighted. We were up against a very difficult situation and we didn't win. But to hell with this business of saying the generals done us dirt."

When Terence Robertson wrote critically about the raid in his 1963 book *Dieppe: The Shame and the Glory*, Lt.Col. Merritt was outraged. "You can wipe out the shame," he was quoted as saying at the time. "It is to the everlasting credit of the Canadian soldier that every man got off the landing craft and went ashore. In neither the planning nor the performance need anyone be ashamed."

When he died on July 12, 2000, in his native Vancouver, his death received national and international coverage. He is buried in Mountain View Cemetery in Vancouver.

Canadian Mortgage and Housing Corporation named a street in Toronto's Topham Village after him. Merritt Road is part of the war veterans housing built in that subdivision after the war.

The Merritt family donated the colonel's Victoria Cross and other military and civic medals to the Canadian War Museum in Ottawa.

As for his heroics during the disastrous attack on the French port, the citation accompanying his Victoria Cross includes these words: "For matchless gallantry and inspiring leadership whilst commanding his battalion during the Dieppe raid. To this Commanding Officer's personal daring, the success of his unit's operations and the safe re-embarkation of a large portion of it were chiefly due."

Captain Frederick Thornton Peters: The Once and Future Hero

Frederick "Fritz" Peters wasn't one to rest on his laurels. He had already fought a war — and had been highly decorated for his efforts — yet here he was once again going into battle at the age of 53 on what everyone agreed could easily turn out to be a suicide mission.

Born on September 17, 1889, in Charlottetown, PEI, the son of the attorney general and first Liberal premier of that province, Fritz Peters moved with his family to British Columbia in 1897. After completing his Canadian education, he successfully pleaded with his parents to allow him to join the Royal Navy at age 16 in 1905, and he subsequently graduated from naval school in England as a midshipman. Three years later, he received his commission as a sub-lieutenant. During World War I, Fritz Peters received the Distinguished Service Order, the first ever given to a Canadian, and the Distinguished Service Cross, for gallantry in action.

That would seem to be enough of a contribution for one family to make to its homeland, especially since Fritz's brother, Gerald Hamilton Peters, had also served in World War I and had died on June 3, 1916. However, when World War II began, Fritz Peters, a career sailor, was quick to heed the rallying cry of "Ready aye ready" and soon found himself once again in the thick of battle.

On July 11, 1940, a grateful Royal Navy added a Bar to the Distinguished Service Cross Peters had been awarded in World War I, once again for meritorious devotion to duty. Little wonder then that this courageous individual would have no qualms about volunteering for a mission fraught with danger.

The wheels for this mission were set in motion when France surrendered to Nazi Germany in December 1940, and Hitler put a puppet French government in place in the Vichy area of the conquered country. This new regime decided to send 14 French warships for safekeeping to the Mediterranean port of Oran, Algeria.

Fearful that the vessels would eventually be used against them, the Allies made the port one of the targets in Operation Torch, the British-American amphibious invasion of northwest Africa scheduled to begin at midnight on November 8, 1942. The exercise involved the landing of American troops around Casablanca while a combined British/American invasion party attacked in the Oran area, and a British unit landed at Algiers.

Part of the Oran assault would be a naval breakthrough of the harbour's defences so that American commando teams could seize the French ships at anchor. The plan, which Captain Peters helped devise, was code-named Operation Reservist, and called for two lightly armed former US Coast Guard cutters, HMS *Hartland* and HMS *Walney*, to breach the port defences.

These 1700-ton sloops were pressed into service for the Oran raid as floating battering rams. The plan was to take the port without damaging strategic facilities by prior bombardment. This meant that troops would be landed by surprise on nearby beaches with orders to encircle the city. The *Walney* and the *Hartland* would then crash the log boom at the harbour entrance, land 400 troops of the 6th US Armored Infantry Division on the waterfront, and prevent the defenders from sabotaging port facilities and scuttling the ships. The landing force included specialists equipped with canoes to bring them quickly alongside the French ships and prevent the ships from being blown up by the Vichy troops.

Many of those involved in the planning of the raid were less than enthusiastic about its chances for success. They pointed out that the assault ships would be without any support until the invading ground troops had reached Oran, and that the harbour was strongly fortified with coastal batteries and shore units with automatic weapons. Furthermore, should the invaders be successful in ramming the entrance boom, they would then face a flotilla of warships manned by French forces whose loyalties were unknown.

But the pro-attack contingent among the planners made a tactical error that nations bent on "liberating" other countries often make. They expressed confidence that the French forces, bristling under the rule of Nazi puppets in the Vichy regime, would provide only token resistance at most, and perhaps even open-armed cooperation when the Allies arrived.

Also in their favour, the plan's advocates argued, was the element of surprise. The ships could break through the barrier and execute their mission before the defenders knew what was happening. On both counts, they were in for a bitter surprise.

Plans for the attack on the Port of Oran included an escape clause where the two cutters were to retreat if the unexpected happened and the French defenders put up strong resistance. Nevertheless, when Vichy French forces dug in their heels and fought ferociously to repel the invasion, Captain Peters received orders to proceed.

The result was a fiasco. As the two cutters, both under the command of Captain Peters, neared the port, harbour defence batteries bathed them in daylight-simulating beams of powerful searchlights and opened fire. Captain Peters, realizing that the crucial element of surprise was lost and that the mission was doomed to failure, called upon his 37 years of naval experience and rammed the log boom across the port entrance anyway, charging into the harbour. Unfortunately, his worst fears materialized and the French warships, including a destroyer and a cruiser, began firing at the two invading craft at point-blank range.

Captain Peters, in an action that has been described as one of the great episodes of naval history, managed to keep the *Walney* on course until a French shell penetrated her boiler and the resulting explosion killed most of the crew. With the small craft engulfed in flames and French firepower lambasting the vessel from all directions, Captain Peters managed to reach the jetty, even though he was blinded in one eye. The *Walney* sank at wharfside with her colours flying. The *Hartland* suffered a similar fate. As those opposed to the plan had feared, the French defenders of Oran methodically destroyed the port facilities and scuttled several ships to block the harbour — the very acts of sabotage the doomed mission was supposed to prevent.

All, however, was not lost. The French sloop *La Surprise*, which had earlier inflicted heavy damage on the *Walney*, made it out of the harbour into open water but was sunk by another member of the invading fleet, HMS *Brilliant*. Four French destroyers tried to slip away in the confusion but met stubborn resistance from a number of British warships. Three of the French vessels were sunk and the fourth was forced back into port.

Captain Peters, who had been blown overboard by the force of an exploding French shell, was captured by Vichy troops at the port and incarcerated in the town jail. Two days later, victorious American troops released him from captivity and the townspeople, having been told that he had been the squadron commander of the two attack vessels, carried him on their shoulders through the streets while admiring crowds pelted him with flowers.

But Captain Peters's euphoria was to be short-lived. The next day, he boarded a Sunderland flying boat for a triumphal return to England. The aircraft crashed off the coast at Plymouth and Captain Peters's body was never found.

In addition to the Victoria Cross, Captain Peters was posthumously awarded the US Distinguished Service Cross — the highest decoration for bravery that the Americans can award a foreign service person.

Because he was a native of Charlottetown, a Naval Reserve building in the PEI capital is named in his honour.

Captain Peters's name appears on the naval memorial at Portsmouth, England. The memorial is situated on Southsea Common, overlooking the promenade, and is accessible at all times. His name appears on Panel 61, Column 3.

The citation accompanying the hero of Oran's VC medal reads, in part: "Captain Peters was in the 'suicide charge' by two little cutters at Oran ... [He] led his force through the boom [blocking the harbour] in the face of point-blank fire from shore batteries, destroyers, and a cruiser — a feat which was described as one of the great episodes of naval history."

1943

Captain Paul Triquet: A Magnificent Flash of Greatness

Captain Paul Triquet's summation of the situation he and his men were in got right to the point: "There are enemy in front of us, behind us, and on our flanks. There is only one safe place — that is on the objective." Brave words from a man who had just witnessed the slaughter of all the participating officers and 50 percent of the men from his company of the Royal 22nd Regiment (the famous Vandoos) in an earlier attack on a German stronghold.

Captain Triquet obviously figured that the only way to rally the remaining troops against the firepower of Nazi tanks, mortars, and machine guns defending the Sicilian hamlet of Casa Berardi was to show disdain for the enemy. "Never mind them. They can't shoot," he shouted above the din of battle as he urged his men forward.

In an action on December 14, 1943, that would later be described as "a magnificent flash of greatness," the 33-year-old Triquet led the reorganized company, supported by tanks from the Ontario Regiment of Oshawa, through a heavily fortified gully that had been the stumbling block to taking Casa Berardi. During the skirmish, four enemy tanks were destroyed, and several enemy machine-gun posts were knocked out.

Casa Berardi was still in German hands, however, and it had to be taken if the key road junction on the main Ortona-Orsogna lateral was to be secured. The Nazis were aware of the small village's strategic importance and had poured infantry troops and tanks into the area with orders to stop the Canadians at all costs.

A career soldier who had inherited his father's love for the military, Captain Triquet was uniquely suited to the job at hand. Born in Quebec City on April 2, 1910, he had joined the Cadet Corps, which his father had organized and trained, while attending Cabano Academy. He enlisted as a private in the Vandoos at the age of 17 and rose rapidly through the ranks. When World War II broke out, he was ready for some serious action, and that's exactly what he got. He sailed for Europe with the Royal 22nd Regiment in December 1939.

With tank backup, Captain Triquet and his men slugged their way to a strategic position on the outskirts of Casa Berardi, but at a tremendous cost — the strength of the company under Triquet's command was reduced to 2 sergeants and 15 men. Anticipating the inevitable counterattack by the Germans, Triquet organized his few remaining troops into a defensive perimeter around the four surviving tanks of the Ontario Regiment and issued the order to stop the advancing enemy: "They shall not pass."

German tanks and infantry hurled themselves at the little band of Vandoos time and again. Captain Triquet seemed to be everywhere during these attacks, going from man to man to offer encouragement and using any weapon at hand to repulse the Nazi advance. He grabbed weapons from the hands of his fallen men — rifles, machine guns, and grenades — to make up in firepower what he had lost in manpower. Witnesses attested that their captain was personally responsible for stopping several advancing German soldiers in their tracks.

In his own report following the battle, Triquet wrote that from time to time he would jump onto one of the Canadian tanks and drop gravel down its open turret to get the attention of the tank commander in the din of battle. He would then point out targets for the tank to knock out.

The Vandoos managed to hold their position all through the night of December 14 despite constant attacks by the enemy. It was later reported that throughout the entire operation Captain Triquet showed utter disregard for danger. His cheerfulness and tireless devotion to duty were a constant source of inspiration. He even dodged enemy fire to visit with a soldier at a lonely outpost.

He was also praised for his tactical skill and leadership

in organizing his company of Vandoos, which had been reduced to a mere handful of combatants. He was able to form his remaining men into a cohesive fighting unit that continued its advance against bitter resistance and held the ground gained against overwhelming odds.

The Germans were determined to hold onto Casa Berardi in order to prevent the advance of the Allies in their push toward Rome. They sent their best troops against the Canadians, but were thwarted by the determination of the Vandoos.

Finally, the remainder of the Canadian battalion arrived to relieve Captain Triquet and his weary men. Casa Berardi finally fell to the Allies, and the Vandoos were able to catch a few hours of well-earned sleep. That done, they were ready to face the enemy once again on the slow and bloody advance of the Canadian troops up the Italian peninsula.

Captain Triquet was the first Canadian in the Italian campaign to be awarded the Victoria Cross and the only member of the Royal 22nd Regiment to receive that honour in World War II. He also was awarded France's Chevalier of the Legion of Honour for the same action.

Captain Triquet returned to Canada with his regiment at the end of hostilities and retired from active service in 1947, after 22 years. He served as district sales manager for a forest products company in Quebec until 1951, when he joined the Reserve Army as Commanding Officer of the Régiment de Levis.

In 1954, he became Colonel Paul Triquet, commanding the 8th Militia Group. He retired to Florida and died on August 8, 1980. He is buried in the Roman Catholic section of the Notre-Dame-des-Neiges cemetery in Montreal.

On November 10, 2003, the Quebec government and Veterans Affairs Canada announced the opening of a joint partnership venture, the Paul Triquet Clinic for Post Traumatic Stress Disorder (PTSD) in Sainte-Foy.

In Italy, the Berardi family, owners of Casa Berardi during the Battle of Ortona, maintains a memorial to Captain Triquet outside their cottage — and welcomes many Canadians to the spot every year. One of the Berardis explains it this way: "You never know who is knocking at the door, but if he's a Canadian, he's certainly a friend."

Lieutenant General Sir Oliver Leese, chief of the Eighth Army, wrote to Triquet when his Victoria Cross award was announced: "Your magnificent feat of arms made victory possible. It was essential to the army's plan that your battalion attain its objective. In your leadership, in the bravery and sacrifice of the men who fought so courageously with you, the Canadian people will realize how much their soldiers have achieved."

1944

Major Charles Ferguson Hoey: Firing from the Hip

The late American movie actor John Wayne, whose exposure to military action was limited to the back lots of Hollywood, spent World War II dressing up as a marine and posing for publicity shots — a Thompson machine gun at his hip and a "let's-give-em-hell" look on his face.

While the "Duke's" contribution to the war effort undoubtedly had its propaganda value, a more authentic role model for those snarling, burp-gun-toting soldiers would have been Major Charles Hoey, a British Columbian fighting in the Far East with the 1st Battalion, the Lincolnshire Regiment. During one incident, despite severe wounds to the leg and head, the 29-year-old Major Hoey seized a Bren gun from one of his men under heavy enemy fire while leading the charge up a hill to capture a Japanese position in Burma (now Myanmar).

Born in Duncan, BC, on Vancouver Island on March 29, 1914, Charles Hoey had sailed for England in April 1933 to fulfil a lifelong dream of a career in the British Army. He first enlisted in the West Kent Regiment where he won a cadetship to the Royal Military College at Sandhurst, enrolling there in September 1935.

Hoey graduated from Sandhurst in December 1936 and, after a brief visit home to Duncan, he joined the 2nd Battalion of the Lincolnshire Regiment — later to be named the Royal Lincolnshires following distinguished service fighting in Burma. This was a family affair for him since his maternal grandfather had been promoted to colonel of the regiment at the outbreak of World War I.

Hoey transferred to the 1st Battalion of the Lincolnshire Regiment, which was at that time in India, and sailed there in September 1937. When the battalion was transferred to Burma in 1942, he found himself in the thick of battle against the Japanese. He was subsequently awarded the Military Cross in July 1943 for his outstanding service at Maungdaw during a raid on an enemy position.

In the citation describing the actions that led to the awarding of the Military Cross, Major Hoey was praised for his disregard for personal safety and his imperturbability in the face of all difficulties and dangers. It was suggested that his fearless example was an inspiration to his men and contributed greatly to the success of the attack. The citation concluded with these remarks: "Major Hoey's determination, courage, and skill during the whole of the operation were beyond praise."

When the smoke of battle had cleared, at least 22 Japanese soldiers lay dead or severely wounded. Due to Major Hoey's skilful handling of his force, the number of casualties was remarkably low. Only three of his men sustained injuries.

On February 16, 1944, in a situation reminiscent of the action that won him the Military Cross, Major Hoey's company was part of a force ordered to capture "at all costs" Feature 315, a peak near Ngakyedauk Pass in the Arakan Hills area of Burma. After a gruelling march of several days through jungles, swamps, and enemy-infested hill country, the British troops reached the base of Feature 315. They learned that the hill was protected by more than 40 Japanese troops in pockets all the way to a command post at the summit, ready to rain down a deadline barrage of rifle, machine-gun, and mortar fire as soon as the Brits launched their attack.

Major Hoey ordered his men to follow him up the hill. Grabbing a Bren gun and, firing from the hip, he led the charge, disregarding the hail of enemy bullets that poured into his unit once the Japanese saw them coming.

The British troops suffered severe losses as they followed their commanding officer up the hill. Major Hoey himself was wounded in the head and left leg. His head wound was so serious that he had trouble seeing through the blood streaming into his eyes. Still, firing the Bren gun and shouting encouragement, he carried on up the incline at such a pace that his men had trouble keeping up with him.

Hoey, with only five of his men still on their feet, reached the summit first and killed all the defenders single-handedly with short bursts from his hip-fired machine gun. The major's own wounds proved to be so serious, however, that he died shortly after the battle was won — a few weeks away from his 30th birthday. His younger brother, Lieutenant Trevor Hoey, would die in the D-Day offensive around Caen in Normandy a few months later.

The *Victoria Daily Times* of January 17, 1945, reported that Major Hoey's mother, Mary Rudyard Hoey, was too ill to travel to Ottawa to receive her son's two medals from the governor general, so BC's lieutenant-governor, W.C. Woodward, officiated at a ceremony at Government House in the provincial capital.

The newspaper praised both Major Charles Hoey and Lieutenant Trevor Hoey for their supreme sacrifice and sympathized with Mrs. Hoey as she took part in the ceremony. "All Duncan was with her in thought," wrote the reporter covering the event, "for the Island town is justifiably proud of these two soldiers who were born and brought up there."

Major Charles Hoey's Victoria Cross is on display at the Sabraon Barrack in Lincoln, England. He is buried in Taukkyan War Cemetery, Rangoon, Myanmar in Plot XII, Row M., Grave No. 2.

Part of the citation accompanying Major Charles Hoey's Victoria Cross reads: "Major Hoey's outstanding gallantry and leadership, his total disregard of personal safety and his grim determination to reach the objective resulted in the capture of this vital position."

Major John Keefer Mahony: No Thought of Failure

Most journalists who got "up close and personal" with the enemy in World War II were armed with nothing deadlier than a portable typewriter, microphone, or notebook. But there were those newsmen who chose to trade in their press cards and pencils for a rifle in order to take a direct part in the action rather than just reporting it. One of these reporters who chose to be a fighting soldier rather than a war correspondent was John "Jack" Keefer Mahony.

Jack Mahony was born in New Westminster, BC, on June 30, 1911. After attending high school in his hometown, Jack got a job as a cub reporter with the daily newspaper *The Province* in Vancouver. A boyhood fascination with all things military, and perhaps a desire to augment his meagre income as low man on the journalistic totem pole, resulted in his joining the Westminster militia regiment. His part-time duties there saw him quickly rise through the ranks to officer status.

When World War II broke out, Jack was among the first to enlist for active service, and eventually he found himself in command of "A" Company of the Westminster Regiment (Motor) in the Italian Campaign.

On May 24, 1944, Major Mahony received orders to establish the initial bridgehead across the River Melfa. Looking east across this waterway, the 32-year-old major surveyed a strong enemy force of tanks, self-propelled guns, and infantry holding defensive positions. Shrugging off any danger this posed as just being part of the job, Major Mahony elected to lead his troops in the attack rather than staying behind to direct the action from the relative safety of the company command post.

Although the crossing was made in full view of and under heavy fire from enemy machine-gun nests, Major Mahony impressed his men by demonstrating great coolness and confidence. A defensive tactic as old as warfare itself is to identify the enemy leader and demoralize his troops by killing him off. The Germans certainly understood this, and, seeing the major gesticulating to his troops, they trained much of their firepower on him. Major Mahony would have been well aware of this risk, yet he exposed himself to enemy fire throughout the battle as he made sure that each section took up its proper position on the west bank of the river. He then led the crossing through a curtain of rifle, machine-gun, and mortar fire.

"A" Company established a small bridgehead on ground where only shallow weapon pits could be dug. There they withstood intense enemy firepower for five hours until the remaining companies and supporting weapons were able to cross the river and reinforce them.

Witnesses to the action would later attest that Major Mahony exuded confidence in the outcome of the battle, never once allowing himself or his men to talk of defeat. This, despite the fact that his company was enclosed on three sides by powerful enemy weapons. There was an 88-mm self-propelled gun about 400 metres to the right, a battery of four 2-cm anti-aircraft (AA) guns 90 metres to the left, a Spandau machine gun 90 metres further to the left, and a second 88-mm self-propelled gun just beyond the Spandau.

If that wasn't enough to give the Canadians pause, there was a company of infantry with mortars and light machine guns on the left of the second 88-mm gun. "A" Company was continually under fire from all of these weapons until it managed to knock out the self-propelled equipment and the infantry on the left flank.

Shortly after establishing the bridgehead, "A" Company faced an enemy counterattack of infantry supported by tanks and self-propelled guns. This action was beaten off by the use of PIATs (Projector Infantry, Anti-Tank — a cross between an anti-tank rifle and a bazooka), 50-mm mortars, and grenades. Major Mahony's skill in organizing his defences was credited with stopping the counterattacking troops in their tracks.

The major seemed to be everywhere during the battle. At one point, he stood in the open with a two-man PIAT team, directing their fire at approaching enemy tanks. In another instance, he saw four of his men pinned down by machine-gun fire behind a mound of hay. He ran toward the enemy, throwing smoke bombs to impair their vision long enough for the Canadians to move to safer ground with the loss of only one man.

With company strength reduced to 60 men and all but one platoon officer wounded, Major Mahony was the driving force behind the repulse of a second counterattack. He hobbled from one section to another with words of encouragement despite excruciating pain from a wound to the head and two bullets in his legs. This second unsuccessful counterattack cost the enemy three self-propelled guns and one tank.

Only when the remaining companies of the regiment had crossed the river to relieve his battle-weary men did the major allow his wounds to be dressed. Even then, he refused to be evacuated, preferring to stay with his company.

The forming and holding of a bridgehead across the river was vital to the whole Canadian Corps action. Failure would have meant delay and a repetition of the attack, probably involving heavy losses of men, materiel, and time. It would also have given the enemy a breathing space that could have broken the impetus of the Corps' advance.

Major Mahony was praised by senior officers for never allowing the thought of failure or withdrawal to enter his mind, and infusing his spirit and determination into all his men. At the first sign of hesitation or faltering, the major was there to encourage, by his own example, those who were feeling the strain of battle.

After recovering from the wounds he sustained during the battle of the River Malfa, Major Mahony remained with the Canadian Army until 1962. He served successively as commandant cadet officer of the Western Command, director of publications for the Canadian Army, and assistant adjutant and quartermaster general of the western Ontario area.

On April 5, 1954, Lieutenant-Colonel Mahony went to Washington, DC, as the Canadian Army's liaison officer. He retired to London, Ontario, where he engaged in youth work. He died on December 16, 1990, and, at his own request, was buried without a military funeral. His body was cremated at the Mount Pleasant Crematorium in London, Ontario.

In honour of heroes born in New Westminster, BC, city council has established a practice of naming new streets after them. One of these is Jack Mahony Place.

According to the citation accompanying Major Mahony's Victoria Cross, the great courage he showed would forever be an inspiration to his regiment and to the Canadian Army. It states: "Major Mahony completely ignored the enemy fire and, with great courage and absolute disregard for personal danger, commanded his company with such great confidence, energy, and skill that the enemy's efforts to destroy the bridgehead were all defeated."

Pilot Officer Andrew Charles Mynarski: The Last Salute

With his parachute and flying suit in flames, Pilot Officer Andy Mynarski stood at the escape hatch of the Lancaster bomber and snapped off a final salute to his doomed fellow crew member trapped in the rear gun turret. He then leapt into the dark skies over Cambrai, France, his fiery clothing giving him the appearance of a falling star as he managed to open his damaged parachute and float to earth.

Ironically, the rear gunner, Pat Brophy, would live to tell the tale. P/O Mynarski, on the other hand, would die of the burns he suffered in trying to save his friend.

Andy Mynarski was born in Winnipeg, Manitoba, on October 14, 1916, the second son of recent Polish immigrants. To help support his mother, two brothers, and three sisters after his father's death, the 16-year-old Andy found work as a chamois cutter for a Winnipeg furrier, a job he kept for four years. In 1940, he joined the Royal Winnipeg Rifles, a militia unit, but he wanted to fly, so he enlisted in the Royal Canadian Air Force (RCAF) the following year. Just before Christmas in 1942, he graduated from No. 3 Bomb and Gunnery School at MacDonald, Manitoba. Mynarski's first operational posting was with Number 9 Squadron in October 1943. In March 1944, he replaced another mid-upper gunner in Number 419 "Moose" Squadron, unaware that this would be his last posting.

Pilot Officer Mynarski was generally known to be a quiet fellow whose ready humour only came to the fore once you got to know him. He was also a superstitious sort. On the night of June 12, 1944, the crew of Lancaster VR-A # KB726 was ordered to take off on a mission to destroy a rail marshalling yard in

German-occupied Cambrai, France. This would be their 13th mission together and, ominously, they would be over the target in the early hours of Friday the 13th. On his way to the plane, 27-year-old Pilot Officer Mynarski found a four-leaf clover in the grass at the side of the runway. In what would prove to be an ironic twist of fate, he insisted that his pal, Flying Officer Pat Brophy, the rear gunner, carry it for good luck.

The mission went relatively smoothly until the Lancaster reached the target area. Shortly after reaching the French coast, the aircraft was briefly illuminated by enemy search-lights, but after evasive action, it was again streaking toward its target area in the safety of the darkness.

As the plane began descending to bombing level, it was attacked from below and astern by an enemy fighter, the deadly twin-engine Junkers 88. The "Lankie" burst into flames and lost power in both port engines. Captain Art De Breyne ordered his crew to bail out.

Rear gunner Brophy later described how the hydraulic system that allowed his ball turret to rotate had been shattered by a cannon shell from the German night fighter. At first, he was unable to reach his parachute, which, due to lack of space in the cramped confines of the turret, was located in the main fuselage of the aircraft. He eventually managed to pry the turret doors open a few centimetres, enabling him to retrieve and strap on the parachute, but it was all in vain since he couldn't open the doors wide enough to get out. He was sure he was about to die a horrible death in the glass inferno of his turret.

At that moment, P/O Mynarski was making his way back to the rear escape hatch and noticed his trapped friend. The two men had become chums during their short time together flying dangerous missions over enemy territory. Off-duty, they had accompanied each other on pub crawls, and Mynarski had even bailed Brophy out of jail one night after a fight with other servicemen.

Brophy's report of their last few moments together described how Mynarski had just opened the escape hatch door and was about to jump when he glanced around and spotted his friend through the Plexiglas of the turret.

"One look told him I was trapped," Brophy told *Reader's Digest* in 1965. "Instantly, he turned away from the hatch — his doorway to safety — and started toward me ... Andy ... had to crawl on his hands and knees, straight through the blazing hydraulic oil. By the time he reached my position in the tail, his uniform and parachute were on fire. I shook my head; it was hopeless. 'Don't try!' I shouted, and waved him away."

Mynarski ignored his friend's orders, even though Brophy outranked him, and grabbed a fire axe in an attempt to smash the turret free. It gave slightly, but not enough. Wild with desperation and pain, he tore at the doors with his bare hands but to no avail.

Finally, with time running out, Mynarski realized that he could do nothing. When Brophy again waved him away, he hung his head and nodded. Brophy got the impression his friend was ashamed to leave — in spite of the fact that he had exposed himself to great pain and probable death by what he had already done.

Mynarski had to crawl backwards through the flaming hydraulic fluid, and as he did so, he never took his eyes off his friend, a look of anguish on his face. Brophy said that when Mynarski reached the escape hatch, he stood up and, as he had done many times before under happier circumstances, he came to attention.

"Standing there in his flaming clothes, a grimly magnificent figure, he saluted me," recalled Brophy. "At the same time, just before he jumped, he said something. And even though I couldn't hear, I knew it was: 'Good night, sir'."

Mynarski and five other crew members had bailed out, forced to leave Brophy alone as the Lancaster plummeted to the earth. The trapped rear gunner said what he thought would be a final prayer as the bomb-laden aircraft hit the ground. But it wasn't his time. The impact and the explosion of 2 of the 20 bombs on board shook the turret loose, sending it skidding across the ground like a hockey puck. It smashed into a tree and threw Brophy clear — shaken and bruised but still alive.

His friend and would-be rescuer didn't fare as well. He had landed alive with his flight suit still in flames. French farmers whisked him off to a doctor but shortly thereafter, Pilot Officer Andrew Mynarski died of severe burns to most of his body.

The rear gunner and the five other members of the crew

lived to tell the tale that would bring posthumous honours to Andy Mynarski. Two of them were taken prisoner by German troops while the other four, including Brophy, managed to evade capture.

Brophy had been knocked unconscious in the crash. When he came to, he noticed that his wristwatch had stopped at 2:13 a.m. on Friday, June 13. He began walking across the countryside until he reached Pas-en-Artois, where a 17-year-old farmboy, Paul Cresson, was out delivering milk and took him to the family farm. Brophy was given civilian clothes and sheltered in the barn. He was later turned over to the *Maquis* — the French Resistance — and eventually made contact with British troops on September 1.

Flying Officer Brophy would later say: "I'll always believe that a divine providence intervened to save me because of what I had seen, so that the world might know of a gallant man who laid down his life for a friend."

Pilot Officer Andy Mynarski is buried at the Méharicourt Memorial Cemetery in France, where the grave reference mistakenly identifies him as a British pilot. His body rests in Grave 40. He was the first member of the Royal Canadian Air Force to be decorated with the Victoria Cross in World War II. His VC is on display at the Air Command Headquarters in Winnipeg, Manitoba.

On June 12, 1994, exactly 50 years after the start of that heroic flight over enemy-held France, the City of Winnipeg named a park after Pilot Officer Andrew Mynarski. In the park is a stone cairn with a plaque describing his intrepid effort to save his friend and fellow officer.

In addition, the Canadian War Plane Heritage Museum, at the Hamilton International Airport in Mount Hope, Ontario, has dedicated its refurbished Lancaster bomber as the "Andrew Mynarski Memorial Lancaster." It is one of only two such aircraft still flying.

The citation accompanying Pilot Officer Mynarski's Victoria Cross points out that he must have been fully aware that in trying to free the rear gunner, he was almost certain to lose his own life. "Despite this, with outstanding courage and complete disregard for his own safety, he went to the rescue," the citation continues. "Willingly accepting the danger, Pilot Officer Mynarski lost his life by a most conspicuous act of heroism, which called for valour of the highest order."

Flight Lieutenant David Ernest Hornell: The Sea Shall Not Have Him

David Hornell and his crew aboard the twin-engine Canso were worried about the weather. The amphibious aircraft was tough to handle at the best of times, and these were not the best of times. The weary officers and NCOs bouncing around in the high winds that buffeted their ponderous airplane knew from the experience of others that a sudden squall could send them all to an instant death in the icy seas off Scotland's Shetland Islands.

It was June 25, 1944, and the aircrew on the flying boat,

part of RCAF 162 Squadron, had been on patrol hunting German U-boats in the waters triangulated by the Shetlands, Norway, and Iceland. They were a long way from their base at Wick, Scotland. If the weather worsened, they would have to make for the Shetlands, about 400 kilometres distant, or, even riskier, they might have to fly 800 kilometres to Reykjavik, Iceland, through storms that would have made a Viking sea captain blanch.

Flight Lieutenant Hornell was born in Lucknow, Ontario, on January 26, 1910. He ought to have been back in Toronto making tires for the war effort at the Goodyear plant where he had worked since 1927, teaching Sunday school on weekends, and living a quiet life. At 34 years of age, he was much more advanced in years than the rest of his crew, and had had to use all his persuasive powers to convince RCAF recruiters that he wasn't too old to become a pilot.

The Canso crew had been airborne for 10 hours and had completed its patrol without spotting any enemy submarines. They must have all breathed a sigh of relief when their captain ordered his navigator, Flying Officer S.E. Matheson, to set a course for home. And then Aegir, Norse god of the sea, decided to shake things up a little.

Struggling to keep the heavy flying boat on course, Flight Lieutenant Hornell heard Flight Sergeant I.J. Bodnoff shout over the intercom: "Fully surfaced U-boat five miles on port bow."

Flight Lieutenant Hornell, a veteran of 60 operational missions consisting of 600 hours of flying time, knew how dangerous it was to attack a surfaced submarine. The German U-boats were armed with 37-mm and 20-mm guns mounted for and aft of the conning tower. In this particular case, the skipper of *U-1255* showed his disdain for the lumbering Canso by staying on the surface, his crew standing ready by their guns.

When Flight Lieutenant Hornell brought his aircraft around to port to come up behind the U-boat, the German submarine captain took evasive action by swerving to starboard.

As the Canso again altered course and approached its target, the U-boat opened fire. Hornell swerved his aircraft from side to side to throw off the enemy gunners as he zeroed in to drop depth charges and allow his gun crews to fire on the submarine.

A raging battle ensued, with the Canso gunners making direct hits to the U-boat's conning tower, killing several of the crew. Then the front starboard gun of the flying boat jammed, leaving only one forward gun operable. Suddenly, direct hits from the U-boat's guns ripped two large holes in the aircraft's starboard wing. The Canso began spewing engine oil and the starboard wing caught fire. At any moment, the fuel tanks could explode. The beleaguered crew of the amphibious airplane could see German sailors in the conning tower waving their arms and cheering over their enemy's plight.

Ignoring the danger of imminent immolation and the

intense enemy gunfire, Flight Lieutenant Hornell and his crew pressed on with the attack, managing to straddle the U-boat with perfectly placed depth charges. Their efforts were rewarded by the sight of the submarine's bow lifting out of the water from the force of the twin explosions. The surviving U-boat crew had only a few moments to abandon ship before their craft sank beneath the waves.

But they would have their revenge. With the Canso shuddering violently and the burning starboard wing blazing more and more ferociously, Hornell needed all his strength to hold the flying boat on course, using his skills to gain altitude. With a lurch that rocked the aircraft wildly, the burning engine detached itself from the wing and plunged into the sea. Exhibiting what was later described as "the utmost coolness," the pilot turned the crippled machine into the wind and brought it safely down on heavy swells. There was little cause for rejoicing. Even in late June, the sea temperatures that far north were bitterly cold — and the disabled aircraft was slowly but steadily sinking. There was nothing for the crew members to do but plunge into the icy water before the suction from the submerging Canso pulled them down with it.

Unfortunately, the worst was yet to come. Only one dinghy had survived the inferno of the burning airplane, and it couldn't hold the entire crew. They were forced to take turns, sitting for a spell in the relative warmth of the pitching lifeboat, then slipping into the frigid waters to let their comrades take their place. The rubber craft at one point capsized in the rough seas, and the weary aircrew had to expend a great deal of their waning strength to right it. Two crew members died of exposure and were last seen drifting off into an icy eternity.

After four hours in the glacial waters, the Canso survivors were elated to see a Norwegian Catalina flying boat soar overhead. But spotting a dinghy in high seas is reputed to be even more difficult than finding the proverbial needle in a haystack. Hornell ordered Flying Officer Graham Campbell, the downed aircraft's nose turret gunner, to fire a rocket from his flare gun. The Catalina kept on flying by. Hornell ordered another projectile to be sent up. Still no reaction from the potential rescue craft. "Only one more," Campbell said as he ejected the second spent shell casing. "Fire it," said Hornell.

The downed aircrew watched despairingly as the Norwegian airplane continued on its flight path. Then they broke into weak cheers as the Catalina began to alter course and swing around to where their dinghy was pitching wildly in the high waves.

The Norwegians dropped an airborne lifeboat, but it fell into raging seas about 450 metres downwind and the exhausted men were unable to swim to it. Their disappointment was tempered by shouts of encouragement from their captain who, by this time, was blinded by the blistering salt in the seawater and near the end of his endurance. Hornell's men would later attest that they could not have survived without his never-ending cheerfulness and inspiring leadership.

It took 21 hours before the seas were calm enough for rescuers to reach the dinghy and pull the exhausted aircrew from the bone-chilling waters. But for Flight Lieutenant David Hornell it was too late. Exhaustion and exposure, no doubt exacerbated by the superhuman effort he had put into keeping his men's spirits up, had taken their toll. He was pronounced dead aboard the rescue launch.

Flight Lieutenant Hornell was awarded the Coastal Command's only RCAF Victoria Cross. It is on loan to the Air Command Headquarters in Winnipeg, Manitoba.

He is buried in Lerwick New Cemetery on the Shetland Islands in the United Kingdom. The grave reference is Terrace 7B, Grave 17.

The citation accompanying Hornell's Victoria Cross states: "Flight Lieutenant Hornell had completed 60 operational missions, involving 600 hours' flying time. He well knew the danger and difficulties attending attacks on submarines. By pressing home a skilful and successful attack against fierce opposition, with his aircraft in a precarious position, and by fortifying and encouraging his comrades in the subsequent ordeal, this officer displayed valour and devotion to duty of the highest order."

Squadron Leader Ian Willoughby Bazalgette: The Master Bomber

Ian "Baz" Bazalgette was a gentle man who spent his off-duty hours listening to classical music and growing roses. His men respected him for always looking after their welfare, and his superior officers admired him for his devotion to duty.

He consistently volunteered for the most dangerous missions and he was almost fanatical about making sure each assignment was completed to the best of his ability. That devotion to duty, while admirable, would have dire consequences.

Early evidence of Baz's courage took the form of a Distinguished Flying Cross (DFC) he was awarded on July 9, 1943, after completing a tour of 30 operations in Italy. Held in high regard by all who came in contact with him, he parlayed his DFC into a posting in April 1944 to the elite No. 635 Pathfinder Squadron as a flight commander with the rank of squadron leader. He had already completed his tour of duty and could have elected to take a safe job as a flying instructor for the duration of the war. Instead he volunteered for hazardous Pathfinder duty, piloting one of the aircraft that arrived first at a target area.

Bazalgette soon proved his worth as a "Master Bomber" charged with marking targets for the ensuing main force of attack aircraft. Only the most skilled at finding and marking enemy installations were given these responsibilities. This involved going in early over the target area, identifying the strategic areas to be bombed, and dropping coloured flares, along with their bomb payload, so that following aircraft would have an easier time of spotting the target area.

It was a particularly hazardous assignment because German anti-aircraft forces and enemy fighter planes were relentless in their efforts to shoot down these "Pathfinders" before they could mark the targets.

Ian Bazalgette was born in Calgary, Alberta, on October 19, 1918, the son of an army pensioner. In 1923, his family moved to Toronto, Ontario, where Baz received his early education. The family then relocated to England and the young Bazalgette completed his schooling.

Following in his father's footsteps, Baz received a commission in the Royal Artillery in September 1940, then transferred a year later to the Royal Air Force Volunteer Reserve.

On August 4, 1944, Baz was in command of a Pathfinder squadron given the vital task of setting the parameters for target bombing of a V-1 rocket site at Trossy St. Maximin in northern France. These unmanned missiles, or "buzzbombs" as they were commonly called, were both destructive and demoralizing to the inhabitants of English towns and cities targeted by the Nazis.

Eyewitnesses attested that these flying bombs would come sputtering over an area making noises like a car backfiring. But the moment the noises stopped, the deathly silence that ensued meant the explosive-packed gizmo was plummeting to earth and would soon wreak havoc on the buildings and any living creatures in the vicinity.

In addition, these rudimentary rockets were the forerunners of the more sophisticated V-2s, which, it was feared, could turn the tide of war in the favour of the Nazis at this late stage of the game. It was therefore essential that the rocket sites and their nearby assembly plants be destroyed.

Unfortunately for Baz and his crew aboard the four-engine Lancaster bomber on its way to Trossy St. Maximin, the area had been heavily bombed on the two previous days so the Germans were ready for another attack. As rear gunner Douglas Cameron would later point out: "A solid sea of flak filled the width of the bomb run," knocking out the other Pathfinders, including the two aircraft piloted by the Master Bomber and the Deputy Master Bomber assigned for that raid.

The success of the attack thereby fell on the shoulders of 25-year-old Squadron Leader Bazalgette, and he took this responsibility seriously. In a hail of ground fire from German anti-aircraft batteries, Baz's Lancaster took a number of direct hits, knocking out the two starboard engines and setting fire to the fuselage. The crew's bomb aimer was badly wounded and the mid-upper gunner was overcome by fumes.

Despite the chaos erupting in his aircraft, Squadron Leader Bazalgette used all his flying skills to press on toward the target, marking and bombing it successfully so attack aircraft coming in behind him would have something to aim at in dropping their bombs. The success of the mission has been credited to the bravery and flying skills of Bazalgette and his crew.

But now came the monumental task of getting the Lancaster and all those aboard back to the safety of their home base. Baz seemed up to the task, exhibiting great flying skill as he wrestled with the controls of the crippled aircraft.

At one point, the Lancaster began to spin in a violent dive, but the unflappable pilot was able to bring it back onto a level course.

However, when one of the port engines failed, leaving only a single motor to do the job, there was nothing to do but to order those crew members who could to bail out.

Squadron Leader Bazalgette could have jumped to safety. But that wasn't in his makeup. He elected to stay at the controls in an attempt to save the lives of the two crew members who had not been able to leave the crippled craft — the wounded bomb aimer and the unconscious air gunner.

As one of four crew members who had managed to get free of the blazing Lancaster, Wireless Operator Chuck Godfrey had a front-row seat for what happened next. Suspended in his parachute, Godfrey watched as his skipper wrestled valiantly with the controls of the doomed aircraft. Godfrey's admiration for such flying skills turned to horror, however, as he watched the Lancaster, engulfed in flames, heading for the small French village of Senantes.

Just as it looked as though the blazing aircraft would hit several houses in its path, Squadron Leader Bazalgette managed to turn the Lancaster aside. He then attempted to land in a nearby clearing.

"I could see it all," Godfrey would later report. "He did get it down in a field ... but it was well ablaze and, with all the petrol on board, it just exploded."

Killed instantly in the fireball that erupted were the

two stricken crew members and the young man who had tried so heroically to save their lives — Squadron Leader Ian Willoughby Bazalgette.

The body of Squadron Leader Bazalgette is buried in the village he took great pains to avoid crashing into, at Senantes Churchyard, Oise, France. His grave is located behind the local War Memorial. It is marked with a military headstone and is designated Grave No. 1.

His Victoria Cross, the only one awarded to an Albertan during World War II, is displayed at the Royal Air Force Museum in Hendon, England.

In 1949, a 2438-metre peak in Willmore Park at the headwaters of the Athabasca River near Jasper National Park was named Mount Bazalgette in memory of this heroic flyer.

In 1990, The Nanton (Alberta) Lancaster Society Air Museum dedicated refurbished Lancaster Bomber FM159 in his honour. On hand for the ceremony were Baz's sister, Mrs. Ethel Broderick, and two of his former crew members who owed their lives to his courage and flying skills —Wireless Operator Chuck Godfrey, DFC, and Flight Engineer George Turner.

Flight Sergeant Larry Melling, DFC, who had joined 635 Squadron a month after Squadron Leader Bazalgette, was also at the dedication ceremony. He recalled being impressed by his superior officer on his first day at the squadron when he walked into the Flight Office.

"He had a tremendous sparkle in his eye is the best

way to describe it," said Melling. "He stood out amongst the people who were there. He was an inviting sort of person, a person that you wouldn't hesitate to approach. He was always the first to volunteer for a job, no matter what sort of job it might be. Even though he was a Squadron Leader, he wasn't above pushing a car to get it started or pumping up someone's bicycle tire."

The citation accompanying Squadron Leader Bazalgette's Victoria Cross bears out Flight Sergeant Melling's testimony, reading in part: "His heroic sacrifice marked the climax of a long career of operations against the enemy. He always chose the more dangerous and exacting roles. His courage and devotion to duty were beyond praise."

Major David Vivian Currie: Closing the Gap

The date was August 18, 1944. Temperatures were soaring close to 40 degrees Celsius, and the acrid fumes of battle and the stench of death fouled the air. The Germans were on the run in northern France and it had begun to dawn on everyone involved that an Allied victory was all but inevitable.

The Nazis had one slim hope. About 300,000 German troops had been trapped in what would go down in history as the Falaise Pocket, south of the Norman city of Caen. There was a gap in the Canadian lines through which the enemy — the Fifth Panzer Army under General Hasso van Manteuffel and the Seventh Army commanded by Feldmarschall Günther von Kluge — was attempting to escape to fight another day.

Canadian Lieutenant-General Guy Simonds was ordered to close the Falaise Gap, and he selected the South Alberta Regiment, under Lieutenant-Colonel Gordon "Swatty" Wotherspoon, to get the job done. Colonel Wotherspoon in turn gave an important part of the assignment to the man he considered to be his most capable officer, Major David Currie.

Currie had been born in Sutherland, Saskatchewan, on July 8, 1912. He learned his trade as an automobile mechanic and welder in Moose Jaw. In 1939, he signed up for part-time duty with a militia reserve unit. Then, in January 1940, he enlisted in the regular army with the rank of lieutenant. He was promoted to captain in 1941 and to major in 1944.

That August, Major Currie was given the assignment to block a main road and prevent the Germans from escaping the encirclement that was gradually drawing a noose around Adolf Hitler's plans for a 1000-year Reich. Currie found himself in charge of a small mixed force of Canadian tanks, self-propelled anti-tank guns, and infantry. By studying the maps and reconnaissance photos of the area, he became convinced that the town of St. Lambert, with its two strategic bridges, was the key to thwarting the enemy. Their tanks and trucks had no other access over the steeply banked River Dives and would have to pass through the town.

The Canadians were ordered to take St. Lambert and hold it, without artillery support, in order to help bring the

German attempt at a breakout to a standstill. The South Alberta's "C" squadron had been badly depleted in earlier battles and could muster no more than 75 officers and men. They were able to augment this number with an under-strength company from the Argyll and Sutherland Highlanders of Canada and a squadron of 15 Sherman tanks, which were inferior in terms of firepower and protective armour to their German counterparts in the area.

Fanatical Nazi troops had taken the town, well aware that they had to hold out until reinforcements arrived to push the Canadians back, so the main force of trapped German troops could escape from the Falaise area.

When Currie's attack force made an initial sortie against the defending Germans, two Canadian tanks managed to enter the town but were knocked out by 88-mm guns. The crews were trapped inside the crippled Shermans but were still able to hold the enemy off with the armoured vehicles' machine-gun and cannon fire.

Realizing it was only a matter of time before the tank crews ran out of ammunition, Major Currie entered the town alone and on foot to reconnoitre the position of the two Shermans just as daylight was fading. Returning to his unit without being spotted by the enemy, he requested and got permission from headquarters to lead a small group of men into the German-occupied town at dusk to try to free the trapped Canadians. Despite heavy enemy mortar fire, Currie's rescue party was able to dash into the town, rifles and machine guns blazing, and extricate the trapped tank crews.

The next morning, Major Currie launched an all-out attack with a small force of Shermans, anti-tank guns, and infantry. So resolute were the defending Germans that it took six hours of heavy fighting to reach the town centre, where Currie's troops were joined by a company of the Lincoln and Welland Regiment and another company of Argylls. But the larger German force held its ground.

One thing the Germans had going for them was the superior punching power of three different classes of German tanks — a Mark IV, a Panther, and the more formidable Tiger, a recent addition to the Nazi arsenal that incorporated and expanded upon the best features of Allied and German armour.

The skill and dogged determination of individual Canadians took care of the tank problem. The Panther was put out of action when Lieutenant Gil Armour of the Argylls climbed onto the turret and dropped a grenade through the hatch. Major Currie's tank, under the direction of the squadron second-in-command Captain John Redden, literally stopped the Mark IV in its tracks with a well-placed shell.

Under the direct command of Major Currie, the massive Tiger tank was also halted. And while his command tank was firing at longer-range targets, the major poked a rifle out the turret to pick off enemy snipers that had come within 45 metres of his headquarters.

Over the next 36 hours, the defending Germans mounted counterattack after counterattack, but Major Currie's defensive tactics allowed his men to stand firm, repulsing each German offensive and causing heavy enemy casualties.

At one point, Major Currie led 40 of the newly arrived reinforcement troops forward as the Germans fell back after another unsuccessful assault. When these new troops panicked under heavy fire and retreated, the major personally rounded them up and led them forward again to a position where they remained until the end of the fighting, inspired by his leadership.

Time and again throughout three days of heavy fighting, his men and his superior officers marvelled at Major Currie's cool demeanour under fire. In one instance, when Canadian artillery had finally become available, their shells were falling within 15 metres of the major's tank. Yet he kept calling for more of the same because of the devastating effect the bombardment was having on the enemy.

At dusk on August 20, the Germans attempted one final assault on the Canadian position, meeting stern resistance that finished them off. Seven enemy tanks, 12 88-mm guns, and 40 vehicles were destroyed, with 300 Germans killed, 500 wounded, and more than 2000 taken prisoner.

Major Currie immediately capitalized on the situation, ordering an attack that completed the capture of the town. This action made certain that the Chambois-Trun escape route the Germans had hoped would be their conduit out of the Falaise Pocket was sealed against them.

Throughout the prolonged battle, the casualties to Major Currie's force were high, yet he never considered the possibility of failure — nor would he allow his men to think about anything but eventual victory. One of Currie's non-commissioned officers would later say: "We knew at one stage that it was going to be a fight to the finish but [Major Currie] was so cool about it, it was impossible for us to get excited."

This fearlessness seemed to drape a cloak of invincibility around the major's shoulders. One of his men later said that the Canadian troops expected at any second to hear that Major Currie, who was taking so many risks, had been killed by enemy fire. "He moved everywhere," said the incredulous soldier. "He would be around the guns and something would land and kill or wound everyone except him. He would be with the infantry and a mortar bomb would get everyone around him. That was happening all the time. His luck was phenomenal — like a poker player getting straight flushes and tights all evening. Everyone felt lucky when he came around."

This luck was also present when a German convoy, belatedly attempting to come to the aid of their embattled Nazi comrades at St. Lambert, ran into an ambush set up by Major Currie and a handful of Canadian soldiers.

As told later by Lieutenant Donald Grant, a Canadian Army photographer who snapped what would become a world-famous picture of the event, Major Currie was quick to take advantage of the situation.

"About 1 p.m., we heard vehicles coming," Lieutenant Grant recalled. "We ducked off the road and along came a motorcycle and sidecar and an armoured half-track full of soldiers — the advance party of a German convoy. They were captured and I got this picture. Before we got the prisoners and the vehicles out of the way, the rest of the convoy came in sight, saw us, and tried to retreat."

While some of the Germans got away, many others were rounded up at gunpoint. Grant estimated that a thousand prisoners were taken that day. And there were so few men with Currie that they couldn't send guards with the Germans. They just headed them back along the road to Trun and told them if they stepped off the road they'd be shot by Canadian snipers in the hills.

During the three days of intense fighting, all the officers under Major Currie's command were either killed or wounded. This meant the major had to be everywhere at once throughout the action. It was later learned that he had been able to catch only one hour's sleep the whole time.

When his force was finally relieved and he was satisfied that the turnover was complete, he fell asleep on his feet and collapsed. After a short rest, however, he was back with his troops, pushing onward toward an ultimate Allied victory.

At the end of World War II, David Currie took a job as equipment superintendent with a paper company in Baie Comeau, Quebec. In 1953, he moved to Montreal and joined a manufacturing company, where he eventually became vice-president.

In 1959, Prime Minister John Diefenbaker appointed Currie Sergeant-at-Arms of the House of Commons, a position of high honour he held for 17 years. He died in Ottawa on June 20, 1986, and is buried in Owen Sound, Ontario.

Major Currie is the third Victoria Cross recipient to be buried in Owen Sound's Greenwood Cemetery — the others being Billy Bishop (Cambrai, France 1917) and Tommy Holmes (Passchendaele, Belgium 1917). Major Currie was the only Canadian awarded the VC during the Normandy invasion in the summer of 1944 who was not killed in the process of earning it.

On August 5, 2004, the city of Owen Sound erected a sidewalk pod memorial in his honour, displaying action photos from his war years and a brief explanation of how he won the Victoria Cross. The heading on the plaque reads: "Owen Sound Local Heroes" and is one of several historical monuments dotted throughout the city.

Major Currie was the only Saskatchewan native to win the Victoria Cross in World War II. (Lieutenant-Colonel Cec Merritt was with the South Saskatchewan Regiment but was born in Vancouver, British Columbia.) The Moose Jaw, Saskatchewan, armoury is named for Major Currie.

A serious, self-deprecating man, Major Currie had been unwilling to go along with Canadian Army public relations officers when, for propaganda purposes after he had been awarded the Victoria Cross, they tried to upgrade his pre-war job as automobile mechanic to manager of the garage. "I just worked there," he would say with a shrug.

Nevertheless, Major Currie displayed the kind of self-control under duress that Canadians can be proud of. The citation accompanying his Victoria Cross reads, in part: "Throughout three days and nights of fierce fighting, Major Currie's gallant conduct and contempt for danger set a magnificent example to all ranks of the force under his command ... There can be no doubt that the success of the attack on and stand against the enemy at St. Lambert-sur-Dives can largely be attributed to this officer's coolness, inspired leadership, and skilful use of the limited weapons at his disposal. The courage and devotion to duty shown by Major Currie during a prolonged period of heavy fighting were outstanding and had a far-reaching effect on the successful outcome of the battle."

Private Ernest Alvia Smith: Contempt for Enemy Fire

It was Ernest Smith's love for travel that brought him close to death on two occasions during the fierce fighting of the Italian campaign in World War II.

Born in New Westminster, BC, on May 3, 1914, Ernie was bitten early by the travel bug. At the age of 16, he left home on a five-year odyssey across Canada, picking up whatever odd jobs he could in those lean Depression days.

With the skills he'd acquired on the road, Ernie went

into the construction business in the late 1930s, but his love of travel kept him dreaming of "those far away places with strange sounding names."

When war broke out in September 1939, a bored and restless Ernie Smith saw his chance to visit some of the sites he'd only heard about from the itinerant men he'd met during his years on the road. An eternal optimist, he never figured he'd actually see any action. He imagined the war would be over in a few months — lasting just long enough for him to get a taste of European wine, women, and song. He was in for a big surprise.

Ernie enlisted in the Seaforth Highlanders of Canada instead of his home unit, the New Westminster Regiment, because, as he put it, he'd heard that many of his former teachers had joined that regiment, and he'd had enough of them during his school years. This irreverent attitude and disrespect for authority would see him busted back to private time and again during his days as a soldier.

Instead of spending his army time lounging around the cafés of Europe, "Smoky" Smith (the name of a movie cowboy hero at the time) found himself wading ashore with the Seaforth Highlanders in Sicily in July of 1943. Just a little over a month later, near the site of volcanic Mount Etna, Private Smith was seriously wounded in the chest by the blast of a grenade. Flown to North Africa for treatment, he spent several months recuperating, coming close to death on several occasions as his battle-weary body fought valiantly to return to health.

Having been injured so severely, Smoky was offered a return to Canada. His two younger sisters had died due to illness, and it was felt his parents had suffered enough. But Smoky's unpredictable nature kicked in once again and he refused repatriation, saying he preferred to return to his unit.

Life for Canadian soldiers in the gruelling Italian campaign was one of day-to-day hardships, where advances were measured in metres rather than kilometres. A little over a year after Smoky returned to his unit, the 2nd Canadian Infantry Brigade was given the difficult task of establishing a bridgehead on the northwest bank of the Savio River. The Allies were attempting to break into the Po Valley in northern Italy to allow a rapid advance into Austria on their way to Germany and total victory over the Nazi Third Reich. But autumn rains had slowed their progress to a crawl.

The Canadians were dug in on the southeast bank of the river and were sitting ducks for the Nazi guns on the high, muddy banks on the other side. "A" Company of the Princess Patricia's Canadian Light Infantry (PPCLI) had managed to ford the rain-swollen river and establish a toehold below the German guns, but at a tremendous cost. The 16 remaining members of PPCLIs had been pinned down in the mud of the northwest bank for nearly 24 hours.

Just before 9 p.m. on the night of October 21, 1944, troops from the Seaforth Highlanders and the Loyal Edmonton Regiment started across the rapidly rising waterway. Once they had secured a position on the northwest bank, they relieved the beleaguered Princess Pats. Their task of holding the bridgehead was that much more difficult because the soft mud of the riverbanks prevented Allied tanks and anti-tank guns from crossing the flood waters in support of the rifle companies.

As the Canadians were consolidating their position and clearing nearby farmhouses of German infantry and machine-gun positions, the Nazis launched a massive counterattack with four Mark V Panther tanks accompanied by two self-propelled guns and about 30 infantrymen.

The Seaforth's commanding officer, Lieutenant-Colonel Henry Bell-Irving, had a surprise in store for the attacking enemy, who no doubt knew the Canadians had no tanks or anti-tank guns backing them up. What each company did have was a new strategic squad called a tank-hunting platoon. This consisted of 16 soldiers organized in eight PIAT (shoulder-fired mortar) teams. The tactic employed by the platoon was to find a tank, immobilize it by shattering its tracks with Hawkins anti-tank grenades, then blow it up with PIAT-launched explosives.

When the counterattack began, 30-year-old Smoky Smith showed what would later be described as "utter contempt for enemy fire." He crossed an open field with two comrades, dodging shell blasts from German tanks and enemy rifle and machine-gun fire. He helped set up one PIAT-armed soldier in a roadside ditch affording him some cover, as well as a good shot at the oncoming tanks.

Smith then re-crossed the field with the second member of the PIAT team, Private James Tennant, and jumped into another ditch, only to discover that during their mad dash his companion had been wounded. Grabbing the second PIAT, Private Smith stood up in full view of an approaching Mark V Panther, ignoring the machine-gun bullets whizzing all around him. Without the luxury of having a partner who could immobilize the tank with the Hawkins grenades, Smoky took aim and put the gigantic armoured vehicle out of commission no more than 10 metres from where he stood.

Immediately, 10 German soldiers jumped off the back of the Panther and charged the lone Canadian soldier with Schmeisser submachine guns and grenades.

Smoky jumped into the middle of the road with a Thompson submachine gun, killing four Germans and driving the others back. When another tank opened fire and more German troops began closing in, he dove back into the ditch to retrieve spare magazines for his "Tommy" gun from the wounded Private Tennant. He kept up a withering curtain of fire until the enemy withdrew in disorder.

While yet another German tank continued to sweep the area from farther away, Smoky dragged his wounded companion behind a nearby farmhouse where a first-aid station had been set up. Once the injured man was being tended to, Smoky returned to the roadside in case another attack came.

At dawn, it became apparent that the enemy had been routed, and the battalion was able to consolidate the bridgehead position vital to the entire operation. Because of the bravery of men like Smoky Smith, the Canadians eventually captured the city of San Giorgio Di Cesena on their way to total victory in the Italian campaign.

Private Smith, Canada's only surviving recipient of the Victoria Cross, was an enlisted man's idol and an officer's cross to bear. An easy-going, fun-loving individual, he could have been the inspiration for the cartoon character "Beetle Bailey" — until it came time to show his mettle. Then he answered the call to duty with everything he had.

Smoky always loved a good time, and if it meant getting into trouble with his superiors, so be it. He might well have inspired the description of the fun-loving, devil-may-care Canadian soldier that made the rounds during World War II. It was alleged that if you gave a Canadian soldier a bottle of brandy and a motorcycle, and told him Berlin was off limits, he'd be there in a matter of hours.

Time and again during his involvement in World War II, Smoky would commit an act of bravery that would earn him a promotion, only to carry out some rule-breaking prank that would see him busted to private once again — the lowly rank he held at the end of hostilities.

It's not that he was a bad soldier. When the going got tough, Smoky definitely got going, and woe betide the German soldier who got in his way. But you never knew what Smoky would do next. Even when he'd been badly wounded in Italy and offered a ticket home to Canada, he insisted on staying until his wounds had healed so that he could fight another day. And that final battle would make him the only Canadian private to win the Victoria Cross in World War II.

Smoky's reputation for kicking over the traces got him locked up in a jail in Naples once it was announced that he had won the Victoria Cross. Knowing he would find the award a good excuse for partying, the authorities were determined he would show up sober for the pinning on of his medal at Buckingham Palace by King George VI.

When it came time to fly him to England for the ceremony, military police unceremoniously threw him in the back of a jeep and drove him through the streets of Naples looking for a soldier his size wearing a clean Seaforth Highlanders uniform that they could commandeer for Smoky.

Even when World War II ended and Smoky returned to Canada, he wasn't finished fighting for his country. When war broke out again in Korea in 1950, Smoky was ready to go back into the thick of the action, re-enlisting in the permanent force in 1951 after years of working in a photographic studio in his home town following his demobilization in April 1945.

The military, however, wouldn't risk his life during the Korean conflict, telling him that once you've been awarded the Victoria Cross you're not allowed to fight anymore.

"Why didn't you tell me before I rejoined?" he groused good-naturedly. He retired for good in 1964 on full pension with the rank of sergeant.

His passion for seeing the world was finally satisfied

Smoky Smith, Canada's only surviving VC winner, took part in D-Day ceremonies at Beny-sur-Mer in June 2004.

when he and his wife opened a travel agency after his retirement from the army. To this day, he continues to act as an ambassador for the Canadian military, showing up at military ceremonies all over the world in his wheelchair, which he refers to as his "staff car."

Smoky Smith has hobnobbed with royalty and high-ranking politicians, and the honours keep rolling in. His home town of New Westminster named a street after him: Smoky Smith Place. The Canadian Pacific Railway renamed one of its vintage passenger coaches after him. It sits in downtown Vancouver and is filled with Smoky Smith memorabilia that the public can pore over at will.

Smoky was appointed to the Order of Canada in November 1995 and the Order of British Columbia in 2002. As the only living Canadian VC recipient, he was on hand to represent all the Canadian winners of the coveted medal when a commemorative postage stamp was unveiled in their honour at National Defence Headquarters in Ottawa on October 2, 2004.

Then it was off to Cesena, Italy, with Veterans Affairs Minister Albina Guarnieri to present a framed copy of the stamp issue to the mayor of that town as part of the 60th anniversary ceremonies for Canada's — and Smoky's — contribution to the war effort during the Italian campaign.

Seeming to have the stamina — and the amazing good fortune — of a dozen individuals, Smoky Smith was praised in the citation accompanying his Victoria Cross as a man possessing qualities of initiative and leadership. The document concludes with these words about his participation in the Italian campaign: "Thus, by the dogged determination, outstanding devotion to duty and superb gallantry of this private soldier, his comrades were so inspired that the bridgehead was held firm against all enemy attacks, pending the arrival of tanks and anti-tank guns some hours later."

1945

Sergeant Aubrey Cosens: The Man from Porquis Junction

It was a cruel twist of fate that brought Aubrey Cosens from the small northeastern Ontario village of Porquis Junction to a date with destiny in the equally small German village of Mooshof, just over the Dutch border.

If he'd had his way, Cosens would have been flying with the Royal Canadian Air Force (RCAF) and, perhaps, would have had a bad time of it anyway, but that wasn't how the cards would be played.

Born the son of a World War I veteran in another small northern Ontario town called Latchford on May 21, 1921, Cosens moved with his family shortly after his birth to Porquis Junction near Iroquois Falls. He left school in 1938 to work with his father on the railway as a section hand.

But Aubrey Cosens had always wanted to fly and so, in

1939, he left Porquis Junction to travel to the nearest recruitment centre with plans to enlist in the RCAF. His application was turned down. By this time, however, World War II had begun and he decided that he should be part of the action. While the air force wouldn't have him, the army would. He signed up with the Argyll and Sutherland Highlanders of Canada (Hamilton) Regiment and served in Canada, Jamaica, and England.

In the summer of 1944, Cosens transferred to the Queen's Own Rifles of Canada and soon received a promotion from corporal to sergeant. All the pieces had thus fallen into place for his dramatic and fatal rendezvous with a sniper in Mooshof a few months later.

It was the night of February 25–26, 1945, and the tip of the Allied spear had been thrust into German territory from Holland. Needless to say, German troops were even more ferocious than they had been to this point in the war, knowing that they were in a fight to the death to protect their homeland.

Battle-hardened German paratroopers, taking advantage of the winter rains that had turned the flat farmlands on the Dutch-German border into a quagmire, had set up strong points in abandoned farm buildings. They were determined to halt the Allied advance, code-named Operation Blockbuster, at all costs.

One of these key Nazi outposts was situated in the small hamlet of Mooshof, perched strategically on a ridge. The attacking Queen's Own Rifles, as part of the 8th Canadian

Brigade, would have to traverse a muddy slope in full sight of enemy guns to take the village.

It fell to Sergeant Cosens's 16th platoon of "D" Company, backed up by two tanks of the 1st Hussars, to attack three farm buildings in Mooshof where the German paratroopers were solidly dug in, enjoying strong mortar and artillery support. Twice the Canadians charged the stone buildings and twice they were beaten back by heavy enemy fire. The Germans, seeing their opportunity as the Canadians retreated, launched a quick counterattack in which Cosens's platoon suffered a number of casualties, and the platoon commander was mortally wounded.

The 23-year-old Cosens held senior rank over the four other men left alive in his platoon and he immediately took command. Ordering his men to cover him, he ran across 25 metres of open ground under heavy enemy shellfire to reach the one remaining Sherman tank still operative. Without thought for his own safety, Sergeant Cosens leapt onto the armoured vehicle and assumed an exposed position in front of the tank's turret. He then began directing fire against the stone farm buildings despite the risks of either being shot like a sitting duck or being thrown off in the wild ride over the obstacle-strewn terrain and crushed beneath the armoured vehicle's gigantic steel treads.

When the Germans launched another counterattack, Cosens ordered the tank to plunge into the midst of the advancing enemy troops as he fired at them with his Sten gun, killing six of them and scattering the rest. Directing the tank to ram into the nearest farm building, he leapt off the armoured vehicle, rushed inside, and killed or captured all the occupants. Jumping back up onto the tank, Cosens ordered it to ram the second building, where he repeated his one-man rout of those inside. Remarkably, he did the same with the third structure, all the time exposed to intense machine-gun and small arms fire, while the four remaining members of his platoon covered him as best they could.

Cosens is credited with almost single-handedly breaking the determined resistance of the Germans at Mooshof and capturing a position that was vital to the success of the future operations of the brigade. It is estimated that he personally killed at least 20 German paratroopers and captured as many more. But, unfortunately, he overlooked one man. A German sniper still hiding in one of the gutted farmhouses drew a bead on Sergeant Cosens and shot him through the head. The man from Porquis Junction died almost instantly on the muddy battlefield of Mooshof.

Sergeant Aubrey Cosens is buried at the Groesbeek Canadian War Cemetery in Holland. His grave reference is VIII H. 2. On the cemetery memorial are inscribed the following words: *Pro amicis mortui amicis vivimus*, which, loosely translated, mean "We live in the hearts of friends for whom we died."

Back home in Canada, his name lives on in the form of the steel-arch Sergeant Aubrey Cosens VC Memorial Bridge on Highway 11 near his birthplace of Latchford, Ontario. Also on Highway 11, just south of its junction with Highway 67 at Porquis Junction — where the Cosens family settled after moving from Latchford — is a plaque describing the heroic actions of this VC winner.

Included in the citation accompanying Sergeant Aubrey Cosens's Victoria Cross are these words: "The outstanding gallantry, initiative and determined leadership of this brave NCO, who himself killed at least 20 of the enemy and took an equal number of prisoners, resulted in the capture of a position which was vital to the success of the future operations of the Brigade."

Major Frederick Albert Tilston: We Held

Major Freddie Tilston's first command under enemy fire was also his last. But he packed more heroics into those few hours than most soldiers demonstrate in an entire war.

Born in Toronto, Ontario, on June 11, 1906, Frederick Albert Tilston was educated at the Ontario College of Pharmacy and the University of Toronto. In 1930, he joined Sterling Drugs as a salesman and moved to the company's headquarters in Windsor, Ontario. By 1936, he had risen to the position of sales manager of the Bayer Aspirin division.

His colleagues at the time would have found it hard to imagine that this mild-mannered sales executive for a drug manufacturing company would one day sustain multiple wounds while leading a charge against overwhelming odds, but that was Freddie Tilston.

In fact, his fellow U of T graduates took it in stride when he enlisted in the army as a private at the outbreak of World War II, suggesting among themselves that "Freddie Tilston would never make an officer." Their smugness turned to surprise, however, when because of his age, education, and experience, he was quickly promoted to sergeant and then to officer status.

In the spring of 1945, the 2nd Canadian Division had been ordered to break through the strongly fortified Hochwald Forest defence line, the last German bastion west of the Rhine River. Nazi troops were ferocious in their defence of this high-ridge country, realizing that they were the last hold-outs against an Allied occupation of their homeland. Once Allied troops crossed the Rhine, the total defeat of Adolf Hitler's Third Reich would be swift.

The Essex Scottish Regiment's role in the upcoming battle was to breach the defence line northeast of the town of Udem, and to clear the northern half of the forest to allow the balance of the brigade to pass.

Just after 7 a.m. on March 1, the attack was launched, and the Canadians realized they had made a serious miscalculation. The torrential spring rains had turned the area into a thick mud slough, with the softened ground unable to support the weight of Sherman tanks. The Canadian troops would have to go into battle without armoured backup.

This was Major Tilston's first battle as commander of

"C" Company of the Essex Scottish, and he received the news of the bogged-down tanks with his usual stoicism. Firing his Sten gun in short, deadly bursts, the 38-year-old major led his troops across 500 metres of open field under heavy enemy fire. He also kept his men close to the bursting shells from Canadian artillery to get maximum cover from the barrage.

Reaching the outer perimeter of the enemy lines, Major Tilston and his troops had to cut through three metres of barbed wire to gain access to the German trenches where a bloody battle flared. When the platoon on the left of the major's position came under heavy fire from an enemy machine-gun post, Tilston dashed forward on his own and silenced the enemy guns with a grenade. He was the first to reach the German position, where he took the first prisoner.

Realizing the importance of keeping up the attack's momentum, Major Tilston ordered his reserve platoon to clear out the remaining enemy while he and a reduced band of men carried on with the main assault.

With the major in the lead, "C" Company once again raced across open ground toward the forest cover where the Germans had dug in. In the bloodbath that followed, Major Tilston sustained a wound to the head that blinded him in one eye and almost took off an ear. Even when enemy fire hit him in the hip, knocking him to the ground, he was only out of action until he could regain his feet. All the while, he kept up a steady stream of encouraging shouts to his men, urging them to press forward and make for the cover of the woods.

Catching up to his company at the edge of the forest, he found the men strung out in a ragged, disorganized line along the front German trench. Despite his wounds, Major Tilston hobbled from man to man, explaining what he wanted each of them to do.

As he quickly scanned the enemy position, Major Tilston saw that the elaborate underground system of dugouts and trenches was heavily fortified. He would have to lead his men in hand-to-hand combat to rout the enemy.

This heroic action under personal duress was an inspiration to his troops, who followed the major as he systematically cleared the area of the determined and savage enemy. In this skirmish, the Canadians overran two German company headquarters and inflicted a number of casualties on the enemy.

So grim had been the battle and so fierce enemy resistance that the company's strength had been reduced to 26 men — one-quarter of its original number. Before the troops could be consolidated, the Germans launched a desperate counterattack, supported by mortar and machine-gun fire. Major Tilston once gain limped in the open from platoon to platoon, organizing their defences and directing fire against the advancing enemy.

With his men running short of ammunition, Major Tilston braved more machine-gun and mortar fire to reach "D" Company some 100 metres away, where he loaded up with grenades and rifle and Bren gun ammunition. He made at least six of these trips within the gunsights of German machine-gun posts. On one of these forays, he grabbed a wireless set to replace his company's damaged radio so that he and his men could re-establish communications with battalion headquarters.

In the heat of battle, Nazi troops got close enough to "C" Company's position to lob grenades into their trenches. But, as would be reported later, Major Tilston's "personal contact, unshakable confidence, and unquenchable enthusiasm so inspired his men that they held firm against great odds."

Finally, Major Tilston's run of luck ended. On one last trip across the shell-raked open area between "C" and "D" Companies, the major was knocked off his feet once again, this time by an enemy mortar shell that severely damaged both his legs. He was found in a shell crater beside the road.

Although very seriously wounded and drifting in and out of consciousness, the major refused medical attention until he had given his one remaining officer complete instructions about his defence plan and had stressed the absolute necessity of holding the position. When medical assistance finally arrived at the shell hole where he lay bleeding profusely, all Freddie Tilston had to say through gritted teeth was: "We held." The badly injured Tilston at last allowed himself to be transported to the rear area, where both his legs were amputated.

Fred Tilston was presented with the Victoria Cross by King George VI in a ceremony at Buckingham Palace in 1945.

After learning to walk with artificial legs and adjusting to the loss of sight in one eye, Major Tilston returned to civilian life in Canada. Exactly one year after the incident at the Hochwald Forest, where he was so severely injured, he returned to his former place of employment, Sterling Drugs.

Shortly after his return, he was named vice-president (sales) and served as president of the company from 1958 to 1970. At the time of his retirement in 1971, he was Sterling's chairman of the board.

In 1963, Fred Tilston became honorary colonel of his old regiment, which had been renamed the Essex and Kent Regiment. He was awarded a knighthood in the Most Venerable Order of the Hospital of St. John of Jerusalem and received an honourary doctor of laws degree from the University of Windsor.

Fred Tilston became honorary director and president of the Canadian Foundation for the Advancement of Pharmacy. He was a director and president of the Proprietary Association of Canada and, in 1965, he was named "Man of the Year" by the Independent Retail Druggists' Association of Montreal.

The VC winner travelled throughout Canada and the world promoting the cause of Canadian war veterans. He also gave assistance to the burn unit installation of Wellesley Hospital in Toronto and worked with young children through the War Amputations of Canada.

Fred Tilston died in the veterans wing of the Sunnybrook Medical Centre on September 23, 1992, at the age of 86. He is buried at Mount Hope Cemetery in Toronto.

After his death, Fred Tilston's family presented his Victoria Cross to the Royal Canadian Military Institute in Toronto.

Major Tilston's actions on that late spring morning in Germany in 1945 were highly praised. The citation he received when he was awarded the Victoria Cross was filled with accolades about his leadership. One sentence in the document sums it up well: "By his calm courage, gallant conduct and total disregard for his own safety, he fired his men with grim determination and their firm stand enabled the regiment to accomplish its object of furnishing the brigade with a solid base through which to launch further successful attacks to clear the forest, thus enabling the division to accomplish its task."

Corporal Frederick George Topham: Toppy's Last Fight

When Fred "Toppy" Topham literally jumped into the thick of battle as a medical orderly with the 1st Canadian Parachute Battalion on March 24, 1945, he had no idea that he was to figure in a very different skirmish more than half a century later — and long after his death.

Corporal Topham was assisting the wounded at a severe firefight east of the Rhine River when he and two other medical aides heard a cry from a downed Canadian soldier lying helplessly in the open. One of Toppy's two companions raced to the stricken man, only to be cut down by German rifle and machine-gun fire as he reached the wounded soldier's side.

Toppy watched, horrified, as the second orderly suffered the same fate.

Despite the loss of his two companions, 27-year-old Corporal Topham didn't hesitate in running to the wounded soldier and picking him up on broad shoulders gained from working in the mines of Northern Ontario. The medic was able to bring the disabled soldier back through heavy enemy fire to the shelter of a nearby wood, even though he himself had been wounded in the face.

Refusing medical assistance, the injured orderly spent several hours administering first aid to the wounded. When all casualties had been tended to, Toppy agreed to have his face wound looked after, and headed back to his company command post. On the way, however, he came across a Bren gun carrier engulfed in flames and, disregarding orders from a nearby officer, braved the imminent explosion of shells from within the vehicle to pull three men to safety. For these acts of bravery, the Toronto-born Toppy Topham received a Victoria Cross.

Corporal Fred Topham's selfless action in saving so many Canadian and British soldiers during action on the east side of the Rhine River on March 24, 1945, was not the first time he had exposed himself to such danger.

Jan de Vries, who served with Toppy during World War II, has written that his comrade's reputation for daring exploits to save wounded soldiers was well established before the incidents in Germany.

De Vries, who spearheaded the drive by the 1st Canadian Parachute Battalion Association to raise enough funds to keep the Topham Victoria Cross in Canada, calls his old friend's entire war record a credit to the battalion.

"I didn't learn about it until we were back in England, but other fellows have told me that he was doing the same thing in France," said de Vries. "The word got around before he ever was put in for the Victoria Cross, and most guys knew what Fred had done."

Corporal Fred Topham was presented with his Victoria Cross ribbon in a military ceremony at Toronto's Exhibition Park on August 2, 1945. Well, at least he was presented with *a* VC ribbon. Because of the war, his own VC was not available at the time of the ceremony. Therefore, Captain Benjamin Handley Geary, who had won a VC with the British Army's East Surrey Regiment at Ypres, Belgium, in World War I, pinned his own ribbon to Topham's uniform.

Fred Topham's nephew, Mike Durrant, has said that his uncle never spoke of his war days. "He was a very shy, humble man," said Durrant. "He did not think he had done anything special. He thought that what he did, anybody else would have done."

In fact, Fred Topham's reticence over his VC award was responsible for what probably still stands as a record for the shortest career with the Toronto Police Department.

When Fred joined the force after his return to Canada, he expected to be treated like every other new policeman, but the chief issued an order that he was not to be made to pound a beat. Family and friends say the chief insisted on Fred wearing his medal and welcoming tourists to the city. The infuriated police recruit quit the force immediately without having served a day.

A fellow veteran got Fred a job as a linesman with Toronto Hydro. What dozens of German soldiers hadn't been successful in doing, a hydro wire was able to accomplish in 1974. Fred Topham died from electrical burns following an accident on the job.

On November 8, 1980, Fred's widow unveiled a marker in memory of her husband at Toronto's Etobicoke Civic Centre. He is buried in Sanctuary Park Cemetery in Etobicoke.

Unfortunately, another foe — human avarice — isn't as easy to defeat as a flesh-and-blood adversary. It would fester beneath the surface and erupt long after Toppy's death.

The VC winner's widow, Mary, died in 2001 and, since the Tophams had no children, the medal became part of an estate to be shared by 15 of Mary's relatives. A VC winner cannot sell his medal but nothing in the rules prevented anyone who came into possession of the bronze decoration after the recipient's death from putting it on sale. However, no one expected that Toppy's surviving relatives would be willing to sell the precious award to an offshore buyer.

To be fair to innocent parties in this sad affair, some of the beneficiaries wanted to donate the medal to a museum, but unanimous consent was required for this to happen.

Unfortunately, it's apparently impossible to reach agreement on such an unselfish motive when 15 people are involved.

Canadians were stunned in the fall of 2004 to learn that a British collector had offered more than $300,000 for this piece of Canada's heritage and that if the sale went through, the VC medal would leave the country, perhaps to be locked away in a private collection forever.

The would-be owner was thought to be British tycoon Lord Ashcroft, a millionaire and former treasurer of the British Conservative Party. He has a reputation for having the largest private collection of VCs in the world. Many of the acquisitions were made under circumstances similar to the Topham controversy, with people upset that the medals would be taken out of public display.

Lord Ashcroft is believed to have been the successful bidder when a British airman's medal was sold for nearly $600,000 (calculated in Canadian funds) in early 2004. He is also reputed to have paid about $320,000 for a VC won by a Gurkha soldier in 1944, and close to $289,000 for a Victoria Cross awarded to a British officer during the Indian Mutiny in 1857.

Canadians of all ages and from all walks of life rallied to a call from the 1st Canadian Parachute Battalion Association to keep the Topham medal in Canada.

Battalion Association President Jan de Vries initiated "The Corporal Fred Topham VC Project" and worked tirelessly to stir up as much publicity about the situation as possible. He was so successful that the beneficiaries, feeling the wrath of the Canadian people, agreed to accept $300,000 in Canadian funds if that amount could be raised.

Schoolchildren across Canada donated pennies, nickels, dimes, quarters, and loonies to the cause. "Collectively, we will be helping to preserve an important piece of Canadian history for generations to come," said Michael Coteau, Toronto school trustee and spokesperson for the fund drive conducted by youngsters across the city. "It is important that we remember the sacrifices of those who have gone before us so that we may better appreciate what we have today."

The Canadian Imperial Bank of Commerce kicked in $25,000 to the Parachute Battalion Association's appeal for funds. The Sun newspaper chain laid out the situation to its readers in news stories, editorials, and opinion columns, raising more than $75,000. The City of Toronto — Toppy's birthplace — turned over $25,000 to the cause and Toronto Hydro, where Fred Topham worked for many years after the war, came through with $20,000. The Ontario Trucking Association handed over $10,000, and another $5000 was donated by the Toronto Police Association.

Other major donors included the Ontario Lottery and Gaming Corporation, East York Kiwanis, Canadian Forces Base Borden, members of the Queen's Own Rifles and its association, numerous individual Canadian Legion branches, Korea and other veterans' associations, and the Airborne Brotherhood. Countless individual Canadians also sent donations to the fund.

So great was the response that the money raised soon topped $300,000. Any excess funds are earmarked for other just causes geared to perpetuating the brave deeds of Canada's fighting men and women.

The Corporal Frederick George Topham Victoria Cross medal has found a permanent home in the Canadian War Museum in Ottawa, where it had been on loan for several years.

And so, once again, Toppy Topham was engaged in a battle against incredible odds — and this one he fought successfully from the grave.

As a testament to his courage, the citation accompanying his Victoria Cross reads, in part: "This NCO showed sustained gallantry of the highest order. For six hours, most of the time in great pain, he performed a series of acts of outstanding bravery, and his magnificent and selfless courage inspired all those who witnessed it."

Lieutenant Robert Hampton Gray: The Canadian Kamikaze

Robert "Hammy" Gray was an inveterate gambler with nerves of steel. After flying one of the many dangerous missions he took on as a pilot with the Royal Canadian Naval Volunteer Reserve, he liked nothing better than to relax with his buddies playing a game of craps. Rolling the dice on land, sea, or in the air apparently gave him the adrenaline rush he craved.

The gambles he took paid off both monetarily and militarily. For his brilliant work during the August 29, 1944, attack on the German battleship *Tirpitz* — named for Admiral Alfred von Tirpitz, the architect of Germany's Imperial Navy — in Norway's Alten Fjord, Lieutenant Gray was mentioned in dispatches. His actions were described as "undaunted courage, skill and determination" in carrying out attacks on the battleship.

In July 1945, he was awarded the Distinguished Service Cross for aiding in the destruction of a Japanese ship in the Tokyo Bay area.

But his biggest gamble would come on August 9, 1945, in the Onagawa Wan, a bay on the main Japanese island of Honshu. This time, Hammy's toss of the dice would come up snake eyes — crapshooter slang for a losing roll. Or perhaps he wouldn't have considered it such a stretch of bad luck after all since it awarded him a distinct place in his country's history. He was the last Canadian to date to be awarded the Victoria Cross and the last Canadian service person killed in action in World War II.

Robert Hampton Gray was born in Trail, BC, on November 2, 1917, the son of a Boer War veteran. His family later moved to Nelson, BC, where he received his elementary and secondary school education. A fun-loving student, he made friends easily and showed a strong interest in sports. With an eye on eventually enrolling at Montreal's McGill University for medical training, Gray spent a year at the University of Alberta in Edmonton and two years at the University of British Columbia in Vancouver.

While at UBC, Hammy became heavily involved in fraternity and campus social activities. He was also associate editor of the campus yearbook, the *Totem*, where he met Pierre Berton. The late author remembered Gray as a quiet and thoughtful individual.

In 1940, Hammy was selected as one of 75 candidates for commissions in the Royal Canadian Navy and was one of 13 who qualified as pilots in the Fleet Air Arm. He received his wings and commission as sub-lieutenant in October 1941. By 1944, he was a lieutenant aboard the aircraft carrier HMS *Formidable*.

When victory in Europe was declared on May 8, 1945, most of Canada's armed forces personnel began the demobilization process that would return them to civilian life. However, Canada, because of its geographic position, wanted a presence in the Pacific theatre of war, and the *Formidable* was one of the naval craft that would make waves in that yet-to-be-won battle area.

On that fateful day in August 1945, Lieutenant Gray took off at the head of a force ordered to attack shipping in Onawaga Wan. Arriving at the target area, the Canadian flyers came upon a number of worthy prey, but also found themselves on the receiving end of a heavy fusillade from shore batteries and five Japanese warships.

Undeterred, Lieutenant Gray decided he would take the lead in going after one of the Japanese vessels. "Taking the destroyer first," he radioed. As he pointed his Corsair into a steep dive, the aircraft was hit by an enemy shellburst. "Going in low," was his unperturbed reaction. The Corsair took another hit and burst into flames.

Staying on course, Gray continued his kamikaze-like dive, emulating the Japanese "Divine Wind" pilots who had attacked a number of Allied warships, including the *Formidable*, on suicidal missions in a desperate attempt to reverse the fortunes of war. When he was within 15 metres of his target, he released his bombs, making at least one direct hit. The destroyer exploded in a fireball and sank.

Lieutenant Gray's crippled aircraft continued on its fatal trajectory, crashing into the ocean and carrying the Canadian pilot to a watery grave. Five days later, the Japanese capitulated, still reeling from the dropping of the atomic bomb on Hiroshima on August 6 and the second A-bomb attack on Nagasaki three days later — on the same day that Lieutenant Gray made his self-sacrificing attack. After nearly six years of bloody conflict, World War II was finally over.

On Remembrance Day, November 11, 1980, a solemn ceremony took place in front of the Government of Canada Building in Nelson, BC.

The mayor and members of City Council were on hand as W.O. (Bill) Morrison, executive assistant to federal Public Works Minister Paul Cosgrove, read a document re-dedicating the edifice as the Gray Building. Morrison also handed the mayor a Canadian flag that had flown on the Peace Tower in Ottawa.

The ceremony was held to honour the memory of

Lieutenant Gray — or, more precisely, to right a wrong that an insensitive federal decision-maker had committed. Lieutenant Gray was reputed to have enjoyed a good scrap and he would have been pleased at the events leading up to the re-dedication of the building.

In the glow of honouring Canadian war heroes, the federal government had originally called its new complex in Nelson the Gray Building. However, in the late 1970s, the ruling Liberal Party decided to try to make disgruntled Western Canadians more aware of the contribution of the federal government by renaming all federal structures "Government of Canada" buildings and scrapping any other names that they might have had.

Whoever came up with this idea obviously had not counted on the feistiness of the residents of Nelson. A motion was passed by city council to petition the federal government to change the name back. An alderwoman on council volunteered to take the message to the Public Works minister, who was responsible for all federal property.

The civic representative hit paydirt with her first telephone call, picked up by Morrison late one night in his Ottawa office. The executive assistant was an old Navy man, the branch of the service in which Gray had served, and he immediately started the wheels in motion to have the wrong-headed decision reversed.

Morrison himself received a hero's welcome at the Nelson Legion the night before the ceremony. And a sizeable portion of the city's population turned out for the Remembrance Day parade and re-dedication event the next day.

Lieutenant Gray has no known grave since neither he nor his aircraft were ever found, but his name is inscribed on the Sailor's Memorial in Point Pleasant Park in Halifax, Nova Scotia. The monument is a granite Cross of Sacrifice over 12 metres high, clearly visible to all ships approaching Halifax.

The cross is mounted on a large podium bearing 23 bronze panels, upon which are inscribed the names of more than 3000 Canadian men and women who are buried at sea. An inscription reads: "Their graves are unknown but their memory shall endure."

A singular honour was also paid the naval officer when a cairn and memorial plaque in his memory were erected by the Japanese in Sakiyama Peace Park on Northern Honshu, overlooking the place where he won his Victoria Cross. This action by the Japanese is a rare tribute to a wartime adversary.

Lieutenant Gray's VC is on loan to the Canadian War Museum in Ottawa. The citation accompanying his Victoria Cross includes the following: "For great bravery in leading an attack within 50 feet [15 metres] of a Japanese destroyer in the face of intense anti-aircraft fire, thereby sinking the destroyer although he was hit and his own aircraft on fire and finally himself killed. He was one of the gallant company of Naval Airmen who, from December 1944, fought and beat the Japanese from Palembang to Tokyo."

Epilogue

Two simple words inscribed below a lion standing astride the British crown say it all: "For Valour."

Until the Crimean War, most medals were reserved for the elite officer cadre of the British Forces. A ground swell of public opinion arose for an order of merit open to all ranks. On January 29, 1855, the Duke of Newcastle, secretary of state for war, announced in the House of Lords that a new award would be struck. Eventually it was decided that the medal "shall only be awarded for most conspicuous bravery, or some daring or pre-eminent act of valour or self-sacrifice or extreme devotion to duty in the presence of the enemy."

This new medal would carry the name of the reigning monarch, Queen Victoria, and she and her consort, Prince Albert, took a direct hand in its design. The medal was originally entitled "The Military Order of Victoria," but the prince thought this too long-winded. In pencil on the draft document creating the award, he ran a line through this proposed title and wrote instead: "The Victoria Cross."

The Queen, for her part, didn't like the original notation, "For The Brave," suggesting that this would mean the only brave men in a battle were those who won the cross. Also in pencil, she crossed out the original motto and replaced it with "For Valour."

Each Victoria Cross medal, weighing 4.2 ounces, is still made by the same London jewellers, Messrs Hancocks. The bronze of the medals reputedly comes from Chinese cannons captured from the Russians at the siege of Sebastopol and melted into ingots. These bronze bars are stored at the British Army's Central Ordnance Depot at Donnington, England.

Since its introduction in 1856 as a way of honouring the heroic deeds of those who fought in the Crimean War, this unique medal has been handed out to fewer than 1400 individuals. Ninety-one of these have been Canadians — 70 of whom fought in World War I. The first Canadian to be honoured was Lieutenant Alexander Roberts Dunn, who distinguished himself at Balaclava in the Crimea in the battle immortalized by Tennyson's poem, "The Charge of the Light Brigade." There were also four awarded to Canadians in 1900 during the South African Boer War.

In a strange coincidence involving Canadian VC recipients, three World War I award winners all lived on the same roadway, Pine Street, in Winnipeg, Manitoba. Frederick Hall won his Victoria Cross at Ypres, Belgium, in 1915; Leo Clarke received his honours for heroic action at Pozieres, France, in 1916; and Robert Shankland was selected for the award because of his valiant efforts at Passchendaele, Belgium, in 1917. It is believed to be the only street in the world to have been home to three Victoria Cross winners. The City of Winnipeg has renamed it Valour Road in honour of the three heroes. A bronze plaque has been mounted on a street lamp to tell this amazing story.

Until that moment of truth when a person puts his or her life on the line, it is virtually impossible to decide who has the attributes that will manifest themselves in acts of courage above and beyond the call of duty.

The 16 Canadian recipients of the Victoria Cross in World War II, for instance, were a disparate group of individuals. They ranged in rank from Private Smoky Smith to Lieutenant-Colonel Cec Merritt. Nine of them fought with regiments of the Royal Canadian Army, three were members of the Royal Canadian Air Force, and one each served with the 1st Canadian Parachute Battalion, the Royal Canadian Navy, the British Army, and the Royal Navy.

The first and last Victoria Crosses awarded to Canadians in World War II were for actions against the Japanese. Both of these VCs were awarded posthumously, and the bodies of the two recipients have no known graves. Only eight of the 16 award winners lived to return to Canada while the other eight died in battle or shortly thereafter of wounds or exposure to the elements suffered during the fighting.

Four Canadian VC winners have been singled out for inclusion on "The Valiants" monument on Confederation Square in Ottawa. These include three of the 16 recipients from World War II — Captain Paul Triquet, Pilot Officer Andrew Mynarski, and Lieutenant Robert Hampton Gray

— as well as World War I recipient Captain Joseph Kaeble, who joined the Royal 22nd Regiment in 1916 and quickly won a Military Medal. He received the Victoria Cross near Arras in 1918 when he single-handedly repelled a strong German attack with his Lewis gun. Dying, he shouted: "Keep it up, boys. Stop them!"

The Victoria Cross is the highest decoration awarded to British and Commonwealth troops and takes precedence over all other decorations. It is worn nearest the buttons of the tunic. By tradition, as an expression of the greatest respect, all military personnel stand when a VC recipient enters a room.

It has been estimated that the chance of surviving an action leading to the awarding of a Victoria Cross is one in 10.

Acknowledgements

As with the author's two previous books about World War II in the *Amazing Stories* series, an invaluable source of information and direct quotations from observers and participants was the two-volume *Reader's Digest* account of *The Canadians At War*. Another important resource for this material was Arthur Bishop's *Our Bravest and Our Best.*

The Veterans Affairs Canada website, http://www.vac-acc.gc.ca, was extremely helpful. In fact, the Web provided access to many sites that offer official and personal accounts of wartime events. Some of the particularly useful ones were the Hong Kong Veterans of Canada site at http://www.hkvca.ca, the Canoe site that gives access to a number of Canadian newspapers at http://www.canoe.ca, the Royal Canadian Legion site at http://www.legionmagazine.com, and the War Amps of Canada site at http://www.waramps.ca.

The author is also indebted to Andrew McGillivary, director general of the Communications Division at Veterans Affairs Canada (VAC) and his staff, as well as other VAC department members who were always ready to answer queries.

A vote of thanks also goes to veterans across the country who have lent encouragement through their reaction to the author's first two books about World War II, and especially to those whom the author met during his attendance at the

60th D-Day commemoration ceremonies in Normandy in June 2004.

That trip was made possible through the generosity of Veterans Affairs Canada, Air Transat, Rail Europe, the Osprey Media Group, Maison de la France (French Government Tourist Office), Ashley Searle at the Canadian Embassy in Paris, the Dubos family of Caen, and the Mathieu family of Courseulles-sur-Mer, site of the Juno Beach Memorial.

And finally, the author would like to thank his wife, Gail, for taking time from her own writing to help him with the research for this book.

Photo Credits

Cover: CP Photo; Tom Douglas: page 88; Royal Hamilton Light Infantry: page 29.

Further Reading

Books

Bishop, Arthur. *Our Bravest and Our Best.* Whitby, ON: McGraw-Hill Ryerson Limited, 1995.

Landry, Pierre, Jack MacFadden, and Angus Scully. *Juno Beach.* Toronto: Penguin Books, 2003.

Reader's Digest. *The Canadians at War 1939/45.* Montreal: Reader's Digest Association (Canada) Ltd., 1969.

Swettenham, John. *Valiant Men.* Ottawa: Canadian War Museum Publications, 1973.

Websites

Canada's Digital Collections: http//collections.ic.gc.ca
Canadian Museum of Civilization: www.civilization.ca
Canoe: www.canoe.ca
CBC Archives: http//archives.cbc.ca
The History Net: www.historynet.com
Hong Kong Veterans Commemorative Association:
www.hkvca.ca

The Nanton Lancaster Society Air Museum:
www.lancastermuseum.ca
National Defence — Army: www.army.dnd.ca
National Defence — Canadian Forces: www.forces.gc.ca
Royal Canadian Legion: www.legionmagazine.com
Spitfire Emporium: www.spitcrazy.com
The War Amps: www.waramps.ca
Veterans Affairs Canada: www.vac-acc.gc.ca

About the Author

Tom Douglas is the author of two other books of military history in the *Amazing Stories* series — *Canadian Spies* and *D-Day*. His father, the late H.M. (Mel) Douglas, was a veteran who served with the 19th Field Regiment and was part of the D-Day invasion.

As an elementary school teacher, Tom served with DND Schools Overseas in Metz, France. During that posting, he visited numerous Canadian battle sites and cemeteries in Europe. He left teaching to become a reporter with *The Sault Ste. Marie Star* and has worked in communications ever since. As a reporter, he was selected by DND to tour Canadian bases in Europe on two occasions.

After working with Canadian Press, and serving as publisher/owner of a weekly newspaper in Queensland, Australia, Tom was hired as communications consultant to the Honourable Bennett Campbell, Minister of Veterans Affairs, in Ottawa.

He travelled with the minister and groups of World War I, World War II, and Korean veterans on several pilgrimages involving such battle sites as Vimy Ridge, Normandy, Brittany, Rome, and Seoul. He was also part of a Canadian delegation that was invited by French President Francois Mitterrand to attend Remembrance Day services at the Arch of Triumph.

Tom accompanied Veterans Affairs Minister Campbell to Europe for the 40th anniversary of D-Day in 1984. They took two side trips — one to unveil a plaque in Rome in honour of the Canada/US Special Services force that liberated the Eternal City, the other to Brittany to honour French-Canadian soldiers who had parachuted into occupied France to set up an escape network for Allied personnel. This latter experience was the inspiration for the *Canadian Spies* book.

Tom and his wife, Gail, also a published author with the *Amazing Stories* series, organized a special 50th anniversary D-Day voyage to Normandy on the *Queen Elizabeth 2* in 1994. The ship was entirely taken over by D-Day veterans, their relatives, and military historians, who were entertained onboard by comedian Bob Hope, World War II songstress Vera Lynn, television anchorman Walter Cronkite, and the Glenn Miller Orchestra.

The following year, Tom led a group of Canadian veterans and their relatives on a five-country bus tour of Europe as part of the commemoration of the 50th anniversary of the Allied victory in Europe (VE Day).

In June 2004, Tom attended the 60th anniversary of the D-Day invasion in Normandy as an accredited journalist with the Osprey Media Group. As the son of a D-Day veteran, he was billeted with a French family — Serge, Martine, Melody, and Marjolaine Dubos — in the City of Caen on the Avenue du 6 juin, named in commemoration of the D-Day landings on June 6, 1944.

On Labour Day 2004, Tom was invited to sign copies of his first two books during the closing ceremonies for the old Canadian War Museum on Sussex Drive in Ottawa.

Tom has written speeches for senior officials of DND and Veterans Affairs Canada. He has also interviewed veterans as the basis for several news articles that have been distributed on the Veterans Affairs' website and to newspapers across Canada. He currently serves as copy editor of *The Canadian Military Journal* and is a participant in The Memory Project, speaking to schoolchildren about the meaning of Remembrance Day.

Tom is a member of Branch 114 (Oakville), Royal Canadian Legion.

Amazing Author Question and Answer

What was your inspiration for writing about these World War II heroes?

A life-long interest in the Canadian military fostered by the fact that my father went in on D-Day.

What surprised you most while you were researching the topic?

How brave our VC winners actually were. Also, how young some of them were and how they instinctively disregarded their own safety in order to get the job done.

What do you most admire about the heroes in this Amazing Story?

Their unselfish devotion to duty.

What difficulties did you run into while conducting your research?

As with most historical writing, weeding out fact from error. In several instances, writers whom I respect would differ on basic facts and it took a great deal of time to determine who was right. It's a writer's fear that he or she chose the wrong source and perpetuated an error.

What is your next project?

Probably a book about the Canadians who lied about their age in order to fight. I'd like to delve into their reasons for doing this.

Who are your Canadian heroes?

Well, of course, I'd have to say Tommy Douglas. Also Pierre Trudeau, Stephen Lewis, Canadian war veterans, those who kept things running while the vets were overseas fighting, and all those people who stand up to the mendacity and bombast of those phonies who somehow get themselves into positions of authority.

Which other Amazing Stories would you recommend?

All of them! I'm grateful to the Amazing Stories crew who work so hard to make history come alive in this country. I particularly recommend my wife's new book in the series: *Diana's Rebel Heritage.*

Amazing Places to Visit

Canadian War Museum Le Breton Flats
Ottawa, Ontario

Canadian Military Heritage Museum
347 Greenwich Street
Brantford, Ontario

The Alberta Aviation Museum
11410 Kingsway Avenue
Edmonton, Alberta

Canadian Warplane Heritage
9280 Airport Road
Mount Hope, Ontario

Canadian Aviation Museum Uplands Airport
Ottawa, Ontario

Air Defence Museum
Bagotville, Quebec

Museum of the Regiments
Calgary, Alberta

Royal Canadian Air Force Museum
Trenton, Ontario

National War Monument
Ottawa, Ontario

Aboriginal Veterans Monument
Ottawa, Ontario

Juno Beach Centre
Courseulles-sur-Mer, Normandy, France

Dieppe Beaches
Dieppe, France

Vimy Ridge Memorial
Vimy, France

OTHER AMAZING STORIES

ISBN	Title
1-55153-959-4	A War Bride's Story
1-55153-794-X	Calgary Flames
1-55153-947-0	Canada's Rumrunners
1-55153-966-7	Canadian Spies
1-55153-795-8	D-Day
1-55153-972-1	David Thompson
1-55153-982-9	Dinosaur Hunters
1-55153-970-5	Early Voyageurs
1-55153-798-2	Edmonton Oilers
1-55153-968-3	Edwin Alonzo Boyd
1-55153-996-9	Emily Carr
1-55153-961-6	Étienne Brûlé
1-55153-791-5	Extraordinary Accounts of Native Life on the West Coast
1-55153-992-6	Ghost Town Stories II
1-55153-984-5	Ghost Town Stories III
1-55153-993-4	Ghost Town Stories
1-55153-973-X	Great Canadian Love Stories
1-55153-777-X	Great Cat Stories
1-55153-946-2	Great Dog Stories
1-55153-773-7	Great Military Leaders
1-55153-785-0	Grey Owl
1-55153-958-6	Hudson's Bay Company Adventures
1-55153-969-1	Klondike Joe Boyle
1-55153-980-2	Legendary Show Jumpers
1-55153-775-3	Lucy Maud Montgomery
1-55153-967-5	Marie Anne Lagimodière
1-55153-964-0	Marilyn Bell
1-55153-999-3	Mary Schäffer
1-55153-953-5	Moe Norman
1-55153-965-9	Native Chiefs and Famous Métis
1-55153-962-4	Niagara Daredevils
1-55153-793-1	Norman Bethune
1-55153-951-9	Ontario Murders
1-55153-790-7	Ottawa Senators
1-55153-960-8	Ottawa Titans
1-55153-945-4	Pierre Elliot Trudeau
1-55153-981-0	Rattenbury
1-55153-991-8	Rebel Women
1-55153-995-0	Rescue Dogs
1-55153-985-3	Riding on the Wild Side
1-55153-974-8	Risk Takers and Innovators
1-55153-956-X	Robert Service
1-55153-799-0	Roberta Bondar
1-55153-997-7	Sam Steele
1-55153-954-3	Snowmobile Adventures
1-55153-971-3	Stolen Horses
1-55153-952-7	Strange Events
1-55153-783-4	Strange Events and More
1-55153-986-1	Tales from the West Coast
1-55153-978-0	The Avro Arrow Story
1-55153-943-8	The Black Donnellys
1-55153-942-X	The Halifax Explosion
1-55153-994-2	The Heart of a Horse
1-55153-944-6	The Life of a Loyalist
1-55153-787-7	The Mad Trapper
1-55153-789-3	The Mounties
1-55153-948-9	The War of 1812 Against the States
1-55153-788-5	Toronto Maple Leafs
1-55153-976-4	Trailblazing Sports Heroes
1-55153-977-2	Unsung Heroes of the Royal Canadian Air Force
1-55153-792-3	Vancouver Canucks
1-55153-989-6	Vancouver's Old-Time Scoundrels
1-55153-990-X	West Coast Adventures
1-55153-987-X	Wilderness Tales
1-55153-873-3	Women Explorers

These titles are available wherever you buy books. If you have trouble finding the book you want, call the Altitude order desk at **1-800-957-6888**, e-mail your request to: **orderdesk@altitudepublishing.com** or visit our Web site **at www.amazingstories.ca**

New **AMAZING STORIES** titles are published every month.